THE PHILOSOPHY OF EXPLANATION

When Explaining the Truth about God the Terms Used Are an Indicator of One's Intellectual Maturity

by

James W. Peterson

Dorrance Publishing Co
585 Alpha Drive
Suite 103
Pittsburgh, PA 15238
Visit our website at *www.dorrancebookstore.com*

Paperback ISBN: 979-8-88812-491-8
Hardbound ISBN: 979-8-88812-123-8
eISBN: 979-8-88812-623-3

CONTENTS
THE PHILOSOPHY OF EXPLANATION

SECTION		PAGE
Introduction		v
A Fundamental Truth		vii
Foreword		xi

=============================

*The Greatest Creative Force Known to Exist Anyplace
in the Entire Physical Universe Is the Human Mind.
It Remains Your Intellectual Responsibility to Discover Its Power
and Apply It for Your Happiness and Wellbeing.*

===================================

Chapter 1	The Three Fundamental Types of Sound	1
	Noise	2
	Communication	2
	Language	2
Chapter 2	The Evolution of Language	11
	Real Communication	12
	Insane Ranting	13
	Religious Edicts	14
	Reasoned Understanding	15
Chapter 3	The Evolution of Explanation	19
	Sensing Reality	20
	The source of Real Knowledge	25
	Insane Appearance	21
	Insane Aberration	29
	Religious Acceptance	22
	Religious Faith	31

Reasoned Creation 23

Rational Explanation 34

Explanation 39

Chapter 4 Human Nature 41

Why Does Life Exist 48

Chapter 5 The Science of Philosophy 55

The Science of Philosophy 56

The Philosophical Ladder 58

The What Group 60

The Perspective Group 61

The Explanation Group 62

Chapter 6 Discussing the What Group 65

Chapter 7 Discussing the Perspective Group 79

The Laws of Man 85

Fundamental Capitalism 97

Chapter 8 Discussing the Explanation Group 99

The Truth 101

Chapter 9 The Philosophical Ladder – Revisited 103

Human Nature – Revisited 106

Survival to Happiness 109

Ethical Behavior 110

Moral Interactions 111

Existence 113

Chapter 10 …The God of Capitalism… 119

Personal Salvation 123

Eternal Salvation Via Human Love 125

A Child of God END

Introduction

This book is the result of a father's discovery of the meaning and purpose of his life. It was discovered because of his need to understand it following his daughter's death.

He has discovered that the purpose and course of his life is determined in the same manner as yours. It matters not who you are or what your particular circumstance is. It does not matter if you have lost a child to death. It does not even matter if you have children. It matters not if you are a murderer or a saint, gay or straight, male or female, first-world citizen or jungle tribesman, plant, or animal. The purpose of living is the same for all living things. A rather intriguing claim, isn't it? But it is true just the same, as you will soon discover.

My name is James W. Peterson. This year, 2022, I will be eighty-one years old. I am a retired General Motors Manufacturing engineer living near Lansing, the capital city of Michigan. My wife and I have three children, one of whom died in August of 1980. Her name is Kristin. Her death is my motivation for authoring this book.

If you have experienced the death of a child, my experience is not different from yours in any important way. But the story of how I came about my particular experience may be. We comprise a very special society of humans; we are parents of children who died before we did. It is not supposed to happen that way. Because we did lose a child to death, we are experts in the field of emotional pain, anguish, grieving, sadness, and loneliness. We are not proud, but we realize we have gained knowledge of what life is and how it operates that can be achieved in no other way. We have experienced the very worst pain human beings can experience and remain alive.

It is through their physical experiences that humans acquire knowledge. We have experienced more of what living offers than most people. We, therefore, have more to say about what a happy human existence is and requires.

My struggle began in August of 1980 with Kristin's death. The results of that struggle, i.e., the knowledge I have acquired by consistently applying rigorous rational analysis to the effect of Kristin's death upon my mind, is what I will share with you.

By an Aristotelian style of argument, a truth is said to be that which it is, and it is the same truth for all persons. There is no such thing as a truth that is good for me but is not also good for you; that is called an opinion. Opinions are not truths, and as such they can be false for all who consider them to be true.

Feel free to contact me at: Unclecom2@outlook.com. Please let me know that you have read my book because I, like you, also get many spam emails. If I am still able, I will respond.

A Fundamental Truth

To live, meaning *to continue to survive*, requires recognition that one is a specific kind of living entity—in my case a human being—and as such has specific kinds of survival needs and associated beneficial behaviors. Humans must live in accordance with their nature by acknowledging those laws of nature upon which the achievement of a life proper for a human being depends.

Human beings cannot survive in the way proper for a plant or any of the lower evolved animals, the beasts. In order for humans to survive and achieve the happiness resulting naturally from proper human behavior, they must function as human beings right here on earth. They simply have no other choice or option.

Necessary Background Information

Kristin was born in February 1970. She died in August 1980 at a little more than ten and a half years of age. Kristin died of endocardial fibroelastosis (EFE). EFE is a devastating infantile congestive heart disease that slowly squeezes the life out of its victim. My wife, JoAnn, and I watched Kristin suffer for a year and a half, and then, during the last five days, we waited as the cardiologist tried to find a miracle by which he could save her life. But instead, we had to "request" that the life-support systems be removed.

We Then Stood Beside Her and Watched Her Die.

Kristin was born severely mentally impaired (SMI). To be diagnosed as SMI in Michigan in 1970 meant that Kristin's mind possessed less than 30 percent of what medical professionals perceived as being an average conceptual capability. A person's conceptual capability is a measure of that person's ability to translate reality into intelligence. At her very highest developmental stage, at about her ninth birthday, Kristin was not able to put more than two or three words together to form a sentence. She did not use the toilet; she did not feed herself or dress herself. It is therefore safe to say that she was properly diagnosed as SMI.

Kristen loved football, swimming, circus rides, animals, her older brother Tim and younger sister Tonya, her mother and father, and *especially* her very best friend, a Big Bird doll from Sesame Street, which she carried with her wherever she went. Her best friend was buried with her.

Kristin had a rather keen sense of humor. We often would tease each other and laugh right aloud. I learned very early on that it was necessary that I learn her style of communication, as it was difficult for her to learn mine.

Kristin was every bit as normal a human being as you and me, except that she learned new information very slowly. Humans are different from the other animals in this way. Humans learn and apply new information in their quest to achieve their purpose.

Kristin had a 100-percent normally functioning brain. Meaning that she sensed, identified, and properly integrated herself within the physical world around her, but her learning mind functioned at less than 30-percent efficiency. In other terms, she very slowly learned how to apply the facts of reality for her personal benefit.

It is said that humans are the rational animal, the fundamental distinguishing human characteristic is rationality. Even if Kristin had not died, she would not have learned new information quickly enough to have ever been able to survive independently to achieve her purpose. However, she did function rationally.

I belabor this point for a purpose. It is by applying one's intelligence for understanding what human happiness is and depends upon that is fundamentally important in understanding why humans suffer so much mental anguish at the death of their child. I emphasize *their* child for obvious reasons. All <u>unnatural</u> deaths are especially sad, but the horrendous pain experienced by a parent at the death of their *own* child is inexplicably harsh. It took me twenty years to understand it and an additional twenty-plus years learning <u>how</u> to explain it. If you have lost a child to death the explanation will not make you feel any better about that. However, you will soon understand that you are responding normally and that you aren't going to go crazy as a result of the depth of your own personal emotional pain, anguish, sadness, and loneliness.

Following are myths and untruths uttered by the uninitiated, meaning those who have not lost a child to death. Notice how all myths are based upon the fallacy of a desire for "closure."

"Time heals all wounds."

Baloney! This myth suggests that in time you will learn to "deal" with it. Who could ever believe that dealing with or coming to terms with or becoming more at ease with or feeling better about or more accepting of the death of their child is a true desire of a grieving parent? What a grieving parent wants is to understand the source and the meaning of the pain. They do not want to give up that painful memory of their child to such an irrational premise. All memories of their dead child are treasures of their mind—even, and especially, that last one.

"The pain will go away, and you will be left with nothing but the good memories."

Baloney! A grieving parent *worries* that the pain will someday go away. They worry that they might actually *forget* about their child's worst moment. Can you imagine a more pressing fear than the fear that you might actually forget that? My daughter suffered greatly for one and a half years and then died with great difficulty. The good news I have for you is that I have not forgotten it, and nor will you. The pain is as real today as it was then. I have not forgotten her or her last moments with me, though they are very painful. I still treasure *all* of her memories.

"Your child is in heaven and therefore is no longer sick or in pain."

Baloney! My daughter was sick, very sick. If I were to see her any other way, I would not recognize her. If I could have affected her birth so that she would have been born "normal," I would have. To imply that I did not love her just the way she was is absurd. Please do not believe that any change to my daughter since she has died will somehow reduce the pain of the fact of her death, or that I would want it to.

"You should be over it by now. Perhaps you should be seeking professional help."

Baloney! Unless the professional has also lost a child, there is no way he can understand what my needs are. If the professional has lost a child, he does understand and now realizes that I do not need help. I am upset because my child died. *Duh!*

"God so loves your child that he personally summoned her home to sit by his side in heaven forever. Take comfort in the loving grace of your father, God the Almighty, creator and ruler of heaven and earth."

Baloney! Let him take somebody else's kid. Leave mine here. I love her, too. As a matter of fact, I bet I love her more than he does. I did not kill her, after all, and he did.

FOREWORD

The preceding introduction is a sample of the text of my first book, *The Mind of God*. It was written from the religious perspective of the supernatural existence of a Deity God. *The Mind of God* has been slightly edited to bring certain information up to date. *The Mind of God* reveals a history few persons, and yet too many, have experienced.

My purpose for writing it was purely to chronicle my experience of living with Kristin, loving her as only a parent can, watching her improve, and then watching her die—and resolving the effect this had on the operations of my mind. It is not a well-written book, nor was that, at the time, a concern of mine.

This book is very different. This book is intended to explain how ***The Philosophy of Explanation*** evolved over more than a forty-year period following Kristin's death.

In addition, I am concerned about the mental acuity of some of the intellectuals determining the direction of our nation. They seem to have abdicated their intellect in favor of a lesser standard, the nature of which is difficult to discern. This book will establish reasoned guideposts permitting one to logically understand and then explain any person's intellectual competency—including one's own.

If you consider yourself a religious person, you may have difficulty with what I lay out about my view of religion. You will, however, discover that I am very honest. This honesty may challenge your current religious bias, thus permitting you to pursue a happier path because it may cause you to reevaluate the central religious premises behind why you think the way you do and therefore on the way you behave.

It is not my intent to cause anyone undue pain or suffering. However, I do understand this could happen. I offer no apologies. It remains one's responsibility to think about what one knows to be the case and from there to understand from where one's pain originates. I am not the source of it.

The Greatest Creative Force Known to Exist Anyplace in the Entire Physical Universe Is the Human Mind.

It Remains Your Intellectual Responsibility to Discover Its Power and Apply It for Your Happiness and Wellbeing.

CHAPTER 1

The Three Fundamental Types of Sound

If you were to walk into a forest and stand quietly beside a flowing brook, you would soon become aware of various types of sound.

Noise

You would become aware of the sound produced as the water flows down the brook and as the wind blows though the trees and grasses. This sound has been named: It is called *noise*. *Noise* is the name assigned to naturally occurring sound. Noise results naturally from nature interacting with nature at the inanimate level.

Communication

As you continued to stand there, you would become aware of another type of sound, the sound that the forest animals make. Forest animals purposefully make sound. This purposefully created sound is not called *noise*, it is called *communication*.

Forest animals communicate what they are sensually conscious of by making specific kinds of sounds to denote that it exists. The purpose of animal communication, then, is to vocally symbolize the conscious existence of a sensually known real physical something or relationship. For example, forest animals communicate anger, fear, acceptance, and a desire to mate.

The sounds forest animals make can seem quite noisy to humans because their sounds lack a well-defined or understandable purpose. When the sounds of forest-animal communication lack a known or defined purpose, they revert back to being called *noise*.

Language

Then, as you returned to society, you would become aware of the sounds that humans create. Like all high-functioning animals, humans also purposefully create sound. But purposefully created human sound is not called *communication*. It is called *language*.

Unlike forest-animal communication, the purpose of which is to only vocally symbolize the conscious existence of a sensually known something or relationship, the purpose of human language is to explain the nature of human nature and that upon which its continued happy existence right here on earth depends.

However, and unlike the other animals, humans have the added ability to create visual symbols to denote the existence of the sound symbols they create. Examples of visual symbols humans have created to symbolize the existence of the vocalized sounds of their language are displayed within this very book.

Notice how the way some people use language seems very noisy. These people seem to be using common terms of the human language, but the way they are using these terms leaves us confounded as to what they are actually talking about, or worse, what they believe they are actually talking about. They may believe they are using language in a proper human manner, but they are not.

If one were to speak with another for a long enough period of time, and discuss a sufficiently wide variety of subjects, issues, ideas, and concerns, one would begin to understand where that person's mind spends most of its time. As such, it becomes critical that one's own choice of the terms used to explain something (anything) are well founded in the existence of the absolute nature of physical reality, thus making their meaning universally accurate, true, and verifiable.

Even the human language, when not referencing something known or knowable, reverts back to being called *noise*. To keep this book from being considered *noisy*, I will begin by discussing why humans make certain types of audio/visual symbols called their *language* and then advance that discussion until I get to the sound visually symbolized as *explanation*. Then I will have the material with which to develop a completely new philosophy: ***The Philosophy of Explanation***.

From this foundation, I will be able to explain God. But first we must start with something much more concrete.

Chair

To point and simply utter the sound visually symbolized as "*chair*" requires a much different kind of effort than explaining what the cause of the sound visually symbol as "chair" is.

If one were to point at a certain object in physical reality and then simply utter the sound visually symbolized as *chair*, one's purpose for uttering that sound would be sensually known by another. The other would sensually know what it was one was talking about. The other would know the reason and purpose behind why one created the sound visually symbolized as *chair*.

In this specific instance, one would be acting in a manner similar to the other high-functioning animals. Again, one would simply be vocally symbolizing the sensual nature of the physical characteristics of the object one's brain is conscious of.

If, however, that object is not within the sensual range of the other's brain, then one would need to explain why one uttered the sound visually symbolized as *chair*. This requires an effort of a very different kind.

Prior to being able to explain anything, I must first explain why the audio/visual symbol *explanation* exists. I will begin with the audio/visual symbol *know* and then progress the discussion through *validate* and then through *understand* to finally end up at *explanation*.

Know

For others to know what one knows requires that their brain is also being sensually stimulated by what the existence of the absolute nature of its physical characteristics is.

<u>Here is an important definition</u>: "*Knowing* is that automatically occurring sensual response occurring between two objects when at least one of these objects is a brain." Please note that I will be repeating this important definition through this book.

Knowing that a physical something exists cannot be avoided, controlled, influenced, or in any other way manipulated. But it can be denied. Denial of what is known is a psychological issue and, as such, is outside the philosophical focus of this book.

Try this "knowing" test. Look at a real physical something, an object in reality. Then, without doing anything else, do not know it. Do not know that it actually does exist in a real physical way. It is impossible to not know that a real physical something exists.

To know that a physical something exists is the first, the primary, requirement of being able to explain what it is and how it relates to the known existence of oneself. When one says one knows something, one is saying that that something actually does physically exist, and that any other person can also sensually know that it does. If that something is not within the sensual range of the other's brain, then one has the responsibility of validation.

Validation

To validate that what one is saying is rational requires that another's brain is also able to sensually know that it does physically exist. To *validate* means "to be able to know." Validation is the ability of one's own, or another's, brain to sensually observe that which is claimed to physically exist.

For example, if one were to claim, "There is a large orange orangutan riding around on a unicycle outside this room," validating that claim as rational requires that the claimed existence of the absolute nature of its physical characteristics is able to be sensually known to exist—that is, that it is able to be sensually observed by the sense organs extending from one's, or the other's, brain.

To validate that what one (or another) is saying is rational, one (or the other) must be able to go outside the room and sensually observe that which is claimed to exist there. The requirement is that there actually is "a large orange orangutan riding around on a unicycle outside this room." It must actually physically exist; otherwise, the claim stating it does exist cannot be validated and the claim reverts to noise.

Absent the ability to validate that a claim is rational, i.e., that it is a literal, representation of that which one is claiming to know, one has no option but to consider the claimant to be mistaken, is a liar, is delusional, or perhaps is a believer in the validity of that claim only because it was uttered by someone he or she trusts. The ability to understand what it is that is being claimed to exist is a more fundamental and is therefore a more important issue.

Understand

For another's mind to understand what one is saying requires that his or her mind is able to "conceptually" imagine what the existence of the absolute nature of the physical characteristics of what one is talking about would need to be 'factually' *imaged* within their brain. Did you notice how our focus has changed from *brain* orientation to *mind* orientation with this comment?

Note: It is not proper to claim that the mind function of the human brain can be sensually known to exist. This is because such a claim implies that it exists as a real physical object. When we use the audio/visual symbol *mind*, what we are talking about is a specific functionality of the human brain. Importantly, no other animal has *demonstrated* the existence of that human brain functionality termed *mind*.

To this point we have been dealing with *brain consciousness*. Brain consciousness requires that a brain is being actively physically stimulated. Brain consciousness involves sensually knowing that a physical something exists. Sensual brain knowing is a prerequisite of that same brain becoming factually conscious of what it sensually knows to exist. Evidence of factual consciousness is called an image, a brain-image.

When discussing the idea visually symbolized as *understand*, we must transition from *brain* orientation to *mind* orientation—that is, from brain consciousness to mind awareness. Where brain consciousness deals with the physical nature of brain-sensing, mind awareness deals with the intellectual nature of mental-perception. In other terms, we transition from the physical nature of brain-sensing through the factual nature of conscious imaging to the intellectual nature of mental-perception to eventually end up at the conceptual nature of human intelligence. One demonstrates the perceptual nature of one's intelligence whenever one explains the factual nature of that which one's brain is conscious of.

Where *consciousness* is the ability of a brain to create a fact-based image of that which is physically stimulating it, *understanding* is the ability of that brain's mind function to perceptually identify (meaning to purposefully create the identity of) whatever its brain is able to consciously create a true (a fact-based) image of.

A rational expression flows naturally whenever uttering a reasoned explanation back into reality. For example: The human brain sensually "observes" a something. Its perceptual mind function purposefully "identifies" it. It is after this point that the mind can understand and then from that point explain the factual nature of whatever it is that its brain is sensually observing.

Where sensual *knowing* is a brain focused idea, perceptual *identification* is a mind-focused idea. The transition point between the knowing functions of a brain and the perceptual function of its mind is at **identity**. The objects of reality are factually imaged by conscious brain functions. Their identity is perceptually crafted from the factual nature of their brain images.

One's identity is not automatically sensed by one's conscious brain function, it is purposefully created by its perceptual mind function.

Note that it is the objects of reality that are sensed by a brain to become the facts resulting from that brain's physical experiences. Those facts are what consciousness converts into a true image of whatever it is that is responsible for causing them to exist. Since that brain's images are constructed of fact, then, they (the fact-based images) are considered to be a *true* mental representation of that which is responsible for causing those facts to exist. It is the perceived existence of fact that a brain's mind function utilizes to eventually construct the conceptual nature of its intelligence from.

Conceptual intelligence cannot exist in the absence of perceptualized identity, which cannot exist in the absence of true imaging, which cannot exist in the absence of factual stimulation, which cannot exist in the absence of the **existence** of the absolute nature of the objects in physical reality.

Sensual knowing takes place between a brain and another physical object, whereas intellectual understanding takes place totally within that same brain's mind function. What a brain factually senses is called the **existence** of the absolute nature of the physical characteristics of an *object in reality*; what its mind function utilizes to create its identity from is called the true nature of that same objects *fact-based image*.

Notice how an object's identity does not exist in an absolute physical manner. It exists in an abstract, perceptually understandable, manner. Meaning that an objects identity is purposefully created by a mind from that which its brain's consciousness function factually presents to it in the form of an image. It is in this way that the object's identity can properly be claimed to be objectively based.

For a brain to create a truly formed mental image of a real object requires that the existence of the absolute nature of the physical characteristics of the object exists within that brain in a specific kind of way, as the facts of which the true nature of that objects brain-image ultimately consists of. For that same brain's mind function to perceptually identify what its brain has consciously created a true (a fact-based) image of, requires that the image exists in a specific kind of way, as the <u>knowledge</u> from which "information" about the true nature of its fact-based image can be abstracted. When this is the case, then, that brain's mind function is able to abstract information from knowledge with which to conceptualize the terms upon which its intelligence depends.

The previous is saying that a conceptualized term is the epistemological concomitant of the metaphysical nature of the object responsible for its reasoned creation. It is as if they exist as one and the same. Caution: They are not!

Objects exist physically; the intelligence resulting from them exists conceptually. All objects exist "in reality." The terms resulting from their purpose driven creation exist "in intelligence." Therefore, the terms of intelligence cannot be created in the absence of the **existence** of the absolute nature of the physical characteristics of the objects in reality upon which their intellectual nature depends.

An example: The intellectual nature of the audio/visual symbol *chair* is different from the physical nature of the object upon which its intellectual nature depends. *Chair* is merely the audio/visual symbol created to denote the existence of the absolute nature of the physical characteristics of a specific real object. Its definition describes what it is and how one is related to it. In other terms, it is the definition of the audio/visual symbol *chair* that is its conceptual aspect. Again, *chair* is not intellectual, its definition is. There are audio/visual symbols such as *large*, which are "fundamentally" intellectual. These will be discussed later under the appropriate section.

For now, one must simply acknowledge that for others to understand what one is talking about requires that the terms necessary for their understanding to occur must preexist in their mind. In this case, the terms of *large, orange, orangutan, riding, unicycle, outside,* and *room* must preexist in their mind. When this is the case, these terms can be recalled by their mind and used to imagine (or to reimage) and thereby understand (not sensually know, but conceptually understand) what their brain must become factually conscious of when it is taken outside the room to validate whether what one is saying is rational, i.e., whether it was constructed from what one's brain sensually knows to be the case.

The other's mind compares what its brain has become factually conscious of with that which its mind function has imagined (or reimaged) what its brain must sensually observe. When these agree, then that other's mind has confirmed that one's claim was rationally constructed. That it was constructed from what one sensually knows to be the case. Possessing intelligence is the prerequisite for formulating a reason-based explanation.

Explanation

For others to be able to explain what it is one is talking about requires that their mind is able to think about what the requirements are for it to be considered an explanation.

Their mind must think about, and be able to explain, the requirement that the terms necessary for their understanding to take place must preexist within their mind. They must be able to explain that when this is the case, then their mind is able to understand what it is one is talking about.

Their mind must think about, and be able to explain, the requirement that to validate whether what one is saying is rational, what one is claiming to be the case must actually physically *be* the case. They must be able to explain that when this is the case, then another's brain can sensually know what it is one is talking about and thereby validate one's claim as rational.

Their mind must think about, and be able to explain, the requirement that for another to know what one knows requires their brain is also being physically stimulated by what one's brain sensually knows is the case.

Since I will expect you, when you finish reading this book, to be able to explain God, then I must cause you to have a godly experience, or I must cause you to imagine what a godly experience would need to be if you were to actually experience one. The necessitated rational thinking is your responsibility. I cannot cause you to think rationally and thereby learn how to explain God, or anything else.

When we speak to others there are four alternatives as to how that can and does take place.

CHAPTER 2

The Evolution of Language

Alternative-1a

Real

**The Conscious
State of Existence**

OBJECTIVE

Alternative 1a is the *real* alternative.

This alternative involves the conscious state of existence. This is where things are said to exist as a real something, a physical something, an object.

Under the *real* alternative, the existence of *real* somethings is considered absolute. This is where the absolute nature of real somethings is said to exist physically.

Under this alternative, the physical characteristics of real somethings is sensually known to exist.

This is why this alternative is often called the *objective* alternative.

Alternative-2a

Alternative 2a is the *insane* alternative.

This alternative involves the schizophrenic state of existence. This is where things are said to exist as a *no-thing*.

Under the *insane* alternative, the existence of no-thing is considered demonic. This is where the demonic existence of an insane no-thing is said to be evidence of a serious mental illness.

Under this alternative, the mental nature of the insane existence of no-thing is hallucinated into existence.

This is why this alternative is often called the *emotional* alternative.

Alternative-3a

Real	Insane	Religious
The Conscious State of Existence	The Schizophren: State of Existenc	**The Dogmatic State of Existence**
Something Absolute Physical Known	Nothing Demonic Mental Hallucinated	**Spiritually Hope Mystical Believed**
OBJECTIVE	EMOTIONAL	**SUPERNATURAL**

Alternative 3a is the *religious* alternative.

This alternative involves the dogmatic state of existence. This is where the existence of a no-thing is said to exist *spiritually*.

Under the *religious* alternative, the spiritual existence of dogmatic no-things is hoped to be beneficial to man. This is where the beneficial nature of religious hope is held mystically.

Under this alternative, the beneficial nature of religious hope is simply believed into existence.

This is why this alternative is often called the *supernatural* alternative.

Alternative-4a

Real	Insane	Religious	**Rational**
The Conscious State of Existence	The Schizophrenic State of Existence	The Dogmatic State of Existence	**The Reasoned State of Existence**
Something Absolute Physical Known	Nothing Demonic Mental Hallucinated	Spiritually Hope Mystical Believed	**Idea Intellectual Abstract Proved**
OBJECTIVE	EMOTIONAL	SUPERNATURAL	**SCIENTIFIC**

Alternative 4a is the *rational* alternative.

This alternative involves the reasoned state of existence. This is where things are said to exist as *ideas*.

Under the *rational* alternative, the existence of ideas is considered intellectual. This is where the intellectual nature of ideas is said to exist *abstractly*.

Under this alternative, the abstract nature of an idea can be conceptually proven to be that which it is claimed to be. It is under this alternative that the conceptual nature of ideas is considered to be evidence of intelligence.

This is why this alternative is often called the *scientific* alternative.

Evolution of Language

Real	Insane	Religious	Rational
The Conscious State of Existence	The Schizophrenic State of Existence	The Dogmatic State of Existence	The Reasoned State of Existence
Something Absolute Physical Known	Nothing Demonic Mental Hallucinated	Spiritually Hope Mystical Believed	Idea Intellectual Abstract Proved
OBJECTIVE	EMOTIONAL	SUPERNATURAL	SCIENTIFIC
Symbolic Animal Communication	Fearful Insane Rants	Demanding Religious Edicts	Meaningful Human Language

To this point, we have fairly successfully tracked the evolution of language. Notice how we have moved from the symbolic nature of animal communication through the fearful nature of insane rants and through the demanding nature of religious edicts to end up at the meaningful nature of human language.

Under the REAL Alternative

Non-human animals (the beasts) create sounds to symbolize the existence of that which their brain has consciously imaged the sensual nature of. Beasts communicate that which their brain has sensually imaged by creating a specific sound to symbolize the sensual (not the true) nature of its image within their brain. To humans, most beastly sound seems noisy. It seems noisy only because humans do not understand why it is being created. Oftentimes, a human baby will make sounds that seem noisy for the very reason most beastly sounds seem noisy.

Under the INSANE Alternative

Insane humans use sound in an effort to reveal the existence of that which has no relationship with or to physical nature. Although the sounds of insanity seem familiar, they lack a real application or rational meaning. This is because there seems to be no known purpose or identifiable reason for their use. It is as if the sounds occur in a manner similar to the noise resulting from nature interacting with nature at the inanimate level.

The insane do, of course, have a reason for uttering human-like sound. It is the insane nature of their demons. But since the actual mental existence of these insane demons cannot be verified, their use of human sound seems noisy, that is, without a real cause or rational purpose.

Under the RELIGIOUS Alternative

Religious humans also make human sounds in an attempt to explain the existence of that which has no relationship to or within reality. The religious are attempting to explain the sounds resulting from their "acceptance" of the claims of their trusted religious advisors. However, since these claims have no known source or purpose for their existence, religious persons are considered to be spiritually insane rather than mentally insane. Spiritual insanity is insanity as a result of volitional religious belief rather than by some sort of non-volitional mental impairment.

The religious attempt to explain why it is okay for the sounds they utter to exist absent a known cause or reasoned purpose. Unlike the insane, the religious have no known or verifiable reason for why their sounds exist, and that does not seem to bother them in the least. This is because they have their God on their side. Their God takes the brunt of their insane beliefs permitting them to avoid having to explain the absurdity of their claimed supernatural, spiritual, or mystical cause.

The religious, of course, deny their close link with insanity. But notice that absent a link with reality, they are left with nothing to explain. If a *no-thing* actually did exist, what could be said about it? Nothing! Again notice: The religious have been trying to, and continue to try to, explain the existence of a no-thing. It is as if they are screaming into the darkness of no-place, which also does not exist in either a physical or intellectual manner.

This is evidence of that religiously imposed mental illness called belief. Whether purposeful or not, belief is still evidence of a religiously biased mental illness. Any belief, even when purposefully imposed on oneself by oneself, is an indication of a supernaturally imposed religious bias rather than nonvolitional mental insanity.

Under the RATIONAL Alternative

Rational humans create language as an epistemological tool, a tool to explain reality, necessarily including the reality of happy human existence right here on earth. Knowing what one is talking about takes place in reality, explaining what one understands about that takes place in intelligence.

When *explaining* the nature of human nature to another, the same four alternatives apply, but with added features.

CHAPTER 3

The Evolution of Explanation

Alternative-1b

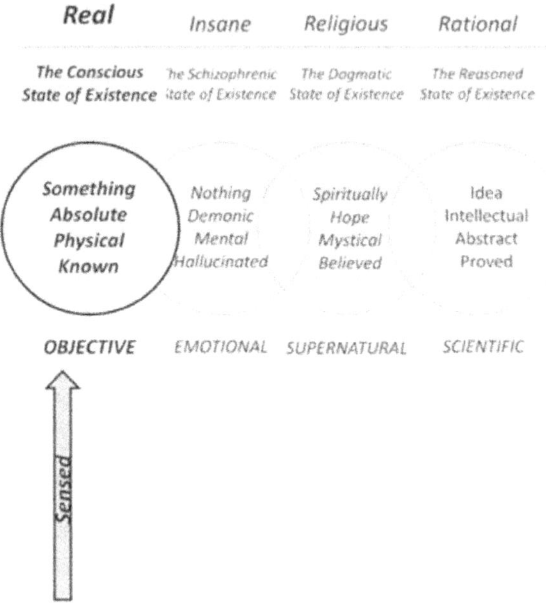

Under alternative 1b, the *real* alternative, it is the absolute nature of the physical characteristics of real objects that is "sensually" known to exist.

It is under this alternative that we discuss how all high-functioning brains operate. All high-functioning brains, necessarily including the human brain, have five sense organs extending from them.

This is how they know that the existence of the absolute nature of the physical characteristics of objects in reality exists. It is sensed.

Alternative-2b

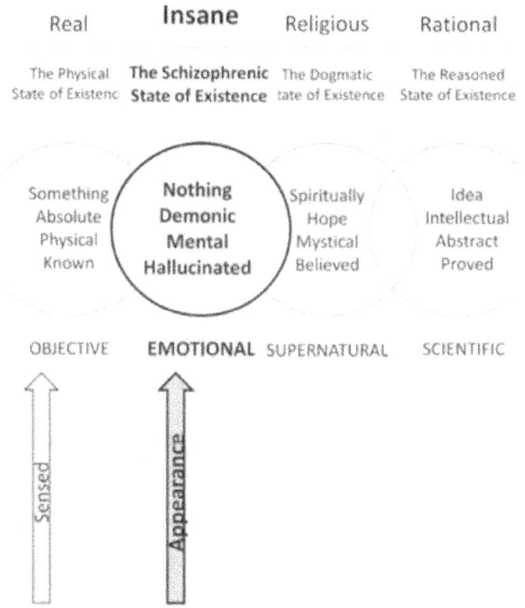

Under alternative 2b, the *insane* alternative, the demotic existence of no-things just seems to appear, as if from nowhere. Rather than being sensually known to exist, as is the case under alternative 1b, the insane appearance of demotic no-things is hallucinated into existence.

To an insane-functioning brain, the hallucinated nature of demons seems to be equivalent to the true nature of factual brain imaging. Where the true nature of an image can be traced to what that brain sensually knows to exist, the hallucinated nature of demons has no known or identifiable cause.

The hallucinated nature of demons is a natural result of a brain that is deranged, meaning electrochemically imbalanced and/or physiologically damaged.

Alternative-3b

Under alternative 3b, the *religious* alternative, the hopeful nature of dogmatic no-things is just simply accepted to be that which one's trusted others have stated they believe it to be.

This premise necessarily requires the associated premise. That the consequence one experiences as a direct result of one's acting based on one's acceptance of the dogmatically stated beliefs of others must also be accepted.

Alternative-4b

Under alternative 4b, the *rational* alternative, the conceptual nature of intellectual things called terms is created. It is created from that which has been validated to be the case. This premise necessarily invokes the associated premise. That one must understand the consequences resulting from acting based on what one understands to be the case prior to initiating the virtues required to bring that understood consequence into reality. Unlike knowing that reality exists, which only involves a brain and, therefore, *is not* discussed under this alternative, creating intelligence also involves mind functionality. Note: It is not until we get to this alternative that we can intelligently discuss the mind function of the human brain.

It is the purpose-driven reasoning power of the human brain's mind function that is responsible for the ability of humans to understand cause-and-effect relationships and to create terms symbolizing that understanding. And it is this ability, the ability to conceptualize what the consequences of one's actions *will* be, that is the reason for why only humans have been able to move themselves from living in caves to living in luxury.

Alternative-1c

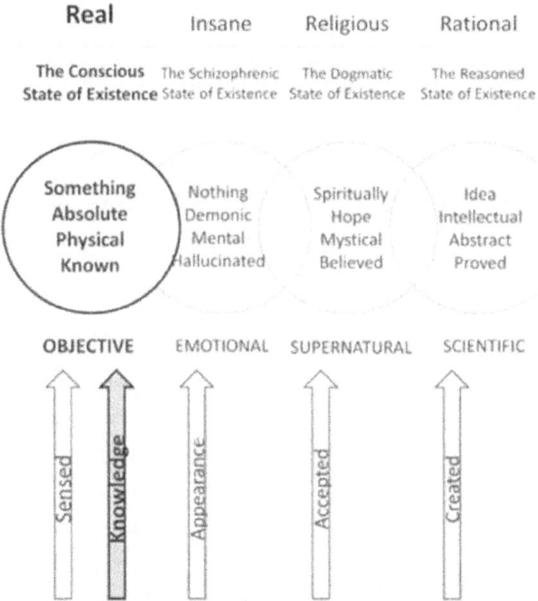

Return again to alternative 1a, the *real* alternative.

It is only under the *real* alternative that we can talk about the *source* of knowledge. The source of knowledge exists **as** being the **existence** of the absolute nature of the physical characteristics of the objects in reality. When we **know** something, this means and requires that our brain is being actively sensually stimulated by the existence of the absolute nature of the physiological and electrochemical nature of the atomic structure of that something's physical characteristics. Meaning that sensually knowing that an object exists requires that the energy field surrounding the atoms of an object is *interfering* with the energy field surrounding the atoms of our brain. When a human brain consciously images the factual nature of that atomic level electrochemical interference, its mind function perceives the naturally resulting brain image to *be* the *knowledge* it requires to identify the cause of it and how it is related to it.

The objects of reality exist physically as billions of atoms. The "*source of the **knowledge**"* required to identify them exists intellectually as a single idea. The source of knowledge, then, is not <u>what</u> physical reality is; it is <u>what</u> the existence of the absolute nature of its *physical characteristics **is***. Said differently, the source of the knowledge necessary for a human mind to explain what the real nature of an object is, and what its relationship to and with it is, is possessed by the object as being the rationally understood existence of, rather than the sensually known <u>*existence*</u> of, the absolute nature of its physical characteristics. First the human brain sensually knows that an object exists, then its perceptual mind identifies its nature. It is from this point that that same mind's conceptual facility can formulate a reason-based explanation.

To validate whether this premise is true, simply look at an object and then close your eyes. You now understand this premise. The source of its knowledge is no longer sensually available to your brain because its atomic structure is no longer electrochemically interfering with the atomic structure of your brain. Your brain no longer sensually knows that the object exists. This test verifies that the source of the knowledge necessary to explain what that object is and what your relationship to and with it is, is the **existence** of the absolute nature of the atomic structure of that object's physical characteristics. Your brain may remember a previous 'sensually potent' atomic level interference, but that is vastly different from it actively sensually knowing *that* it does, in fact, exist.

Note: To state that one's brain sensually knows that a something exists does not imply, as if by the law of necessity, that it has become, or can become, conscious of what it sensually knows to exist. Sensual brain stimulation is a prerequisite of a brain becoming "factually" conscious of what it sensually knows to exist.

Importantly, when speaking epistemologically: It is the **existence** of a human brain stimulation that is called its *fact* by that brain's mind function. Restating: The electrochemical nature of a brain stimulation is perceived to exist "factually" by that brain's mind function. That same mind function *perceives* the existence of the image to <u>**be**</u> factual evidence of the knowledge it requires to identify, understand, and explain why it exists and what its relationship to and with it is.

Follow this logic: Where the physical nature of reality is said to exist absolutely, and its sensual influence on a brain is perceived to exist factually, the factual nature of the resulting brain-image is considered to be a truly formed mental representation of the object responsible for causing the initial brain stimulation to occur. Epistemologically speaking, brain images are considered to be factual evidence of the **knowledge** from which the information necessary for constructing an object's identity is located. It is the total combined set of the *information* abstracted from knowledge that the mind function of the human brain utilizes to formulate "reason-based" ideas about the object responsible for it. It is the resulting reasoned nature of these ideas that is conceptualized into intelligence as terms of language, necessarily including their definitions.

To explain something (i.e., to utter a truth) requires a rational functioning mind; where to simply know something only requires a properly functioning brain. A truth is based on what is understood to be the case by a mind rather than; much more simply, being based on that which is sensually known to exist by a brain.

Human minds purposefully understand cause-and-effect relationships where beastly brains emotionally respond to painful-and-pleasurable experiences.

Whenever one changes the focus of one's interest, the terms one uses to explain that must also change. Otherwise, others will become confused as to what it is one is talking about.

Case in point:

a) When the focus of our interest is only on the <u>inanimate</u> objects of reality, we say the relationship between them is *electrochemical*. Meaning the energy field emitted by the atoms of one is automatically interfering with the energy field emitted by the atoms of the other.

b) When the focus of our interest changes to include the <u>animate</u> objects of reality, we say the "existence" of <u>the</u> exact same *electrochemical* interference is called a *sensual* stimulation.

c) When the focus of our interest changes to include a <u>human brain</u>, we say the "existence" of the exact same *electrochemical* interference is called a fact.

d) When the focus of our interest changes to include a human <u>brain image</u>, we say that the "*existence*" of the exact same *electrochemical* interference exists as being a *truly formed*, or a fact-based, mental representation the absolute nature of the physical characteristics of the object responsible for causing the initial atomic level electrochemical interference to exist.

e) When the focus of our interest changes to include the human brain's <u>mind function</u>, we say that the fact-based existence of the brain-image is perceived to exist by that mind function as **being** the knowledge that it requires to develop and expand its intelligence.

Note that in each case, the fundamental nature of the relationship remains as being the initial electrochemical interference occurring between the atoms of an object and the atoms of a human brain. But since the conditions being discussed are so vastly different, this alone requires us to change the terms we use to discuss them. We do this to avoid becoming confused as to what it is we are specifically talking about.

Alternative-2c

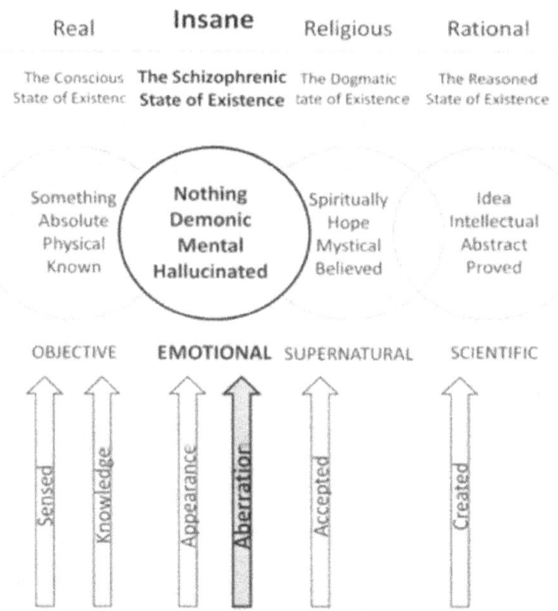

Under alternative 2c, the *insane* alternative, the equivalent to the true nature of brain images, is the insane nature of demonic brain aberrations. Where the *electrochemical* nature of truly formed brain images is evidence of a properly functioning brain, the hallucinatory nature of brain demons is evidence of an insanely functioning brain.

A demonic aberration is a result of the deranged behavior of a damaged brain. The insane existence of demons within a brain is hallucinated into existence rather than being factually imaged by normal brain consciousness. In other terms, hallucinatory demonizing is the insane contrary of conscious imaging.

Conscious brain imaging can only occur within a brain when an object of reality is within the sensual range of the sense organs extending from that brain.

That object's brain-image is consciously formed evidence of the **existence** of the absolute nature of the object's physical characteristics. But notice, it is conscious evidence of the existence of the absolute nature of that brain's physical characteristics as well.

Since a demonic aberration is hallucinated into existence, its cause is not available for scrutiny by the brains of others. In other terms, the non-real (insane or demonic) existence of a mental aberration cannot be validated. It is as if the nonexistence of a *no-thing* actually does exist as a *something* which <u>does not</u> exist. This contradiction is so bizarre it is considered evidence of mental illness. This is why this alternative is often called the emotional alternative.

Schizophrenia is the deluded contrary of consciousness. To be schizophrenic is to not be able to understand the cause of one's mental delusions, of one's demons. Therefore, schizophrenia can be a very scary mental condition.

Alternative-3c

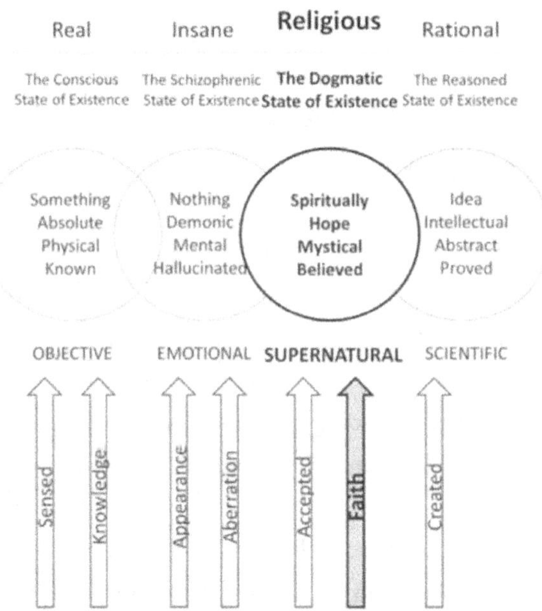

Under alternative 3c, the *religious* alternative, is where we talk about faith. Like schizophrenia, faith can also be considered an abnormal mental condition. And, like schizophrenia, faith is also a fear-based mental condition. For example, "If you don't behave as God says, you are going to go to hell."

Unlike schizophrenia, which is the deluded creation of mental aberrations, faith is a volitional act of religious acceptance. To be religious is to <u>unconditionally</u> accept the dogmatic claims of one's trusted religious advisors. Unfortunately, their claims are based on whatever it is their brain is capable of hallucinating the insane nature of. Religion demands that one simply believe the demonic claims of these trusted others as they continue to attempt to convince one's mind that these are the actual spoken words of their Deity God. Further, religion demands acceptance of the associated consequences.

Where demonic schizophrenia is considered to be a serious brain malfunction, volitional religious acceptance is fully dependent on that spiritually based, but volitional, brain function called **belief**. To a religious mind, the mystical, magical, supernatural basis of spiritual belief supersedes the absolute physical basis of human intelligence. The influence of religious belief on one's thoughts and thereby on one's actions cannot be predicted because it has no known or verifiable foundation. Since the *belief* basis of faith is not founded on known and explained cause-and-effect relationships, then, religious acceptance actually interferers with one's intellectual development and growth.

How else is one to explain why some people purposefully blow themselves up? These people *believe* they are acting in a "proper" human manner. That is why they do that. They can, and do, understand what the actual physical consequence to their living person is going to be. Yet they do it anyway. Why? Because they believe there is going to be a second mystical, spiritual, magical, supernaturally based consequence following the first! Otherwise, they have no reason or purpose for blowing themselves up. From where did they get this absurd notion? They got it from their trusted religious advisors! They got their information as to what proper human behavior is and requires of them from the same kinds of people you may be getting your information from.

Faith is that mental condition where one simply *believes* that others know what it is they are talking about. However, belief in the intellectual efficacy of another's brain is not a means of gaining knowledge. It is the means of becoming and/or remaining ignorant. The faithful are ignorant of that, which is a requirement for humans to achieve happiness right here on earth.

The faithful do not and cannot become faithful by thinking about that which they know to be the case. Under the religious alternative, thinking is considered a blasphemous mental action. Believing (or at least faking to be a believer) is a requirement of staying alive in many cultures dominated by religious theocracy.

The faithful are taught from early childhood to accept the beliefs of their trusted religious advisors. In most cases, this includes their parents. This is why religious people simply accept whatever their trusted religious advisors say is the case, under any condition and all circumstances. One hopes their religious advisors know what it is they are talking about, but they do not. Their information is of a mystical nature, and it is recorded within the texts of religious dogma. Faith-based religious belief can only be acquired by reading religious texts or by accepting the claims of those who claim they have. This is the case simply because it is impossible to sensually observe, and thereby intellectually validate as true, whatever it is the faithful claim to be talking about.

Dogmatically recorded belief, by definition, does not relate to reality. It has no relationship to or with the source of knowledge, and therefore has no intellectual potency. The recorded dogma of any faith exists by result of the spiritual (not hallucinatory) operations of mystically focused minds. Religious dogma exists by result of those faith-based minds that have been able to transition the demons of their hallucinations into the angels of their religion.

By necessity of this self-imposed mental insanity, a religious person can be expected to do and/or say anything and can also be expected to be equally willing to accept whatever the consequence of acting in accordance with whatever his or her faith-based belief is.

Alternative-4c

It is not until we again reach this alternative, the *rational* alternative, that we can begin to explain the nature of human nature and that upon which its happy existence depends.

Explanation requires us to prove a claim is rational, that it is based in what is understood about the sensually known existence of the absolute nature of the physical characteristics of reality. That it is equally valid for every person who has ever lived, for every person who now lives, and for every person who will ever live at any time in the future, anywhere in the entire physical universe.

Under this alternative, the information comprising an explanation is held conceptually. It is held within human *conceptual* intelligence (there is no other kind!). Rather than being *automatically* known to exist, as is the case with the source of the knowledge from which information is abstracted, conceptual intelligence is *purposefully* created by a rational functioning mind. But, recall, it is created from that which a properly functioning human brain sensually knows to be the case.

Recall here, again, that when a human brain knows that a real something exists, this does not imply, as if by the law of necessity, that that brain is factually conscious of what it knows. This same caution must now be expressed with regard to the volitional conceptual transformation of the source of knowledge into intelligence.

Just because the brain-image which the mind function of a human brain perceives to be the **existence** of the knowledge necessary for its intellectual development and growth does not automatically imply, again as if by the law of necessity, that that knowledge has been, will be, or even can be conceptualized into intelligence by that brain's mind function. This depends on how well its conceptual nature is able to function. And this does vary greatly from one individual to another.

Case in point: Recall when I was explaining my daughter's mental condition described as severe mental impairment. Although her brain functioned in a rational manner, its mind function was not able to efficiently conceptualize what it knew to be the case into intelligence. Her conceptual mind functioned at less than 30-percent efficiency even though her conscious brain functioned 100-percent rationally.

Conceptualization of the term -Truth

Repeating:

A truth is not and can never be, not true, i.e., a truth is never false. A truth is always true under all conditions and every circumstance. A truth was true for every person who has ever lived at any time in the past. A truth is true for every person who now lives anywhere on the planet regardless of the conditions where they live or the circumstances under which they live. A truth will remain true for every person who will ever live at any time in the future, anyplace in the entire physical universe.

Again, a brain image is conscious evidence of the existence of the factual nature of an object's physical characteristics on a brain's physical, chemical, and electrical structure. That brain's mind function perceives the existence of the factual nature of a brain image to *be* the knowledge it requires to understand, and from there to explain, how the object will affect one's future existence as a certain kind of living being, a human being.

When the brain-image is verified, by a brain's mind function, to be a truly formed mental representation of the factual nature of the electrochemical effect of an object's physical characteristics on its brain, that same brain's mind function creates a term to denote the existence of (or to intellectually, i.e., to audio/visually, "stand in the place of") the factual nature of that object's physical characteristics and how it must respond to the verified cause of those facts in order to achieve its purpose.

Because the term is verified to have been formulated from a sensually potent physical experience it is considered to be an entity of intelligence. When the totality of such terms is recalled explaining a something (anything) it is the **existence** of the explanation -itself- that is called a **TRUTH.** Therefore, to utter a truth is to reveal the intellectual content of one's mind.

The entities of reality exist absolutely as objects, the terms resulting from their reasoned identification exist abstractly as entities of intelligence. Intelligence, then, is nothing more than reality conceptualized into the terms of language called words and concepts. An example of a truth: The term "reality" explains what is "understood" to be the case with regard to the location of the absolute nature of all objects in the physical universe. They are said to exist "in reality." The term **"truth"** denotes the intellectual nature of that explanation.

It is the factual nature of brain-images that is perceived by a mind to *be* the knowledge it requires for its intellectual development and growth. Meaning, that a brain factually senses the existence of the absolute nature of the physical characteristics of an object and its mind function perceives the *naturally resulting* brain-image to **be** the knowledge it requires to identify what the object is and what its relationship to and with it is. That brain's mind function then abstracts information from that knowledge by which to construct the object's identity. It is an object's identity that is conceptualized into a mind as entities of intelligence.

Importantly, minds do not deal directly with the existence of the absolute nature of the physical characteristics of the entities of reality called objects. That is the specific responsibility of their brain. Minds deal abstractly with the factual nature an object's brain image called *its* knowledge. Stated with other terms, brains selfishly benefit from their ability to successfully deal with the absolute nature of objects. Minds capitalistically profit from their ability to intellectually understand how to invoke the cause-and-effect relationships necessary to experience a proper (a happy) human existence right here on earth. However, the fundamental purpose of a human brain and its mind function is determined by what one's life processes requires of one for it to remain in existence beyond one's lifespan right here on earth.

Since a brain cannot sense *nothing*, then, it cannot become conscious of nothing. When a brain-image seems to exist but there is no physical cause of it, then the actual cause of it is called a *hallucination* and the resulting brain-image is re-termed to become *demon*. A demon is a schizophrenically hallucinated brain existent rather than being a consciously imaged brain existent. Demonic brain activity is not normal, it is insane.

The beastly functioning aspect of a human brain can believe that a brain-image is the existence of an actual real physical something, and its mind function can understand that this is not the case. Note: Brains can believe, and minds can understand. The difference between brain-believing and mind-understanding is the difference between beast and human, between faithful acceptance and reasoned understanding, between schizophrenia and consciousness, between insanity and normalcy, between religion and intelligence.

When one's brain factually senses something, and when one's mind intellectually understands the naturally resulting cause-and-effect relationships, is when one purposefully achieves. Again, with that purpose being determined by what one's life processes require of one's behavior for it to remain in existence, potentially forever.

When discussing inanimate reality, we are concerned with the absolute nature of the naturally occurring electrochemical interference occurring between the atoms of non-living objects. When discussing human brain functioning, we are concerned with the factual nature of that exact same naturally occurring electrochemical interference resulting in the factual nature of brain-images. When discussing human mind functioning, we are concerned with understanding the intellectual nature of the perceived existence of fact-based brain-images termed knowledge. And when discussing ideas, we are concerned with abstracting information from that knowledge with which to construct the identity of the object responsible for causing the initial electrochemical interference to exist. It is the information of which ideas consist of that is conceptualized by that brain's mind function into the terms of human intelligence.

Identity, then, exists as being the "intellectual conduit" through which the information abstracted from knowledge flows into the mind to be conceptualized into the terms of **intelligence**.

Note: The absolute nature of reality is said to exist *objectively*, and the abstract nature of the intelligence resulting from its reasoned identification is said to exist *conceptually*. Intelligence, then, is the epistemological equivalent of the existence of the absolute nature of physical characteristics of the objects of reality. In other terms, conceptual intelligence cannot exist in the absence of the sensually known existence of the absolute nature of the physical characteristics of the objects in reality.

Notice that it is impossible to know nothing. Also notice that much of "modern" science is based on the existence of something that is not known to exist. This is called a theory. Under the insane alternative, this would be called a hallucination. Under the religious alternative, this would be called a *belief*. But here, under the rational alternative, it is called a *theory*.

Be very careful when speaking with a scientist that his explanations are not based on belief but rather on knowledge. The term "religious-scientist" carries a serious, even dangerous, internal contradiction.

The mind of those people who are blowing themselves up is focused on a no-thing as if that is an actual real; a physically existing, something that (rather conveniently for their belief system) does not exist. They deserve what they get—nothing.

Evolution of Explanation

Real	Insane	Religious	Rational
The Conscious State of Existence	The Schizophrenic State of Existence	The Dogmatic State of Existence	The Reasoned State of Existence
Something Absolute Physical Known	Nothing Demonic Mental Hallucinated	Spiritually Hope Mystical Believed	Idea Intellectual Abstract Proved
OBJECTIVE	EMOTIONAL	SUPERNATURAL	SCIENTIFIC
Sensed / Knowledge	Appearance / Aberration	Accepted / Faith	Created / Explained

First, we needed to resolve how sound symbols evolved into language. Now we can use that language to explain how to formulate an *explanation*. To explain something means to provide the source of one's information. Which, in turn, requires knowing what it is one is talking about. "Knowing is that automatically occurring sensual event which takes place between two objects when at least one of those objects is a brain."

An explanation cannot be different from what it is because it is derived from the *existence* of the absolute nature of the physical characteristics of the objects of reality. The often-heard mantra "Let's just agree to disagree" is an absurdity, meaning that it was formulated in the absence of reason. The only position more absurd is one's unconditional acceptance of the religious claim that a **no-thing** (insert deity God) is a something which does not exist in a sensually knowable way—that is, it does not actually physically exist. Therefore (whatever its existence is claimed to be) it must be (it can only be) believed into existence. The only way the claimed existence of a non-real deity God can influence one's mind and therefore one's actions is if its nonexistence is believed to be real.

To explain something is to utter a truth. Which means to reveal one's intelligence. To explain the nature of human happiness is to reveal the laws of nature governing what a proper human existence consists of, necessarily including that upon which its continued happy existence depends upon right here on earth. Explaining the nature of human happiness is, by necessity, done outside the dogmatic boundaries enforced by religious believers. Under certain circumstances, explaining the true nature of human happiness right here on earth can be extremely dangerous.

Some people get so upset; they actually explode!

CHAPTER 4

HUMAN NATURE
Real
Insane
Religious
Rational
The Conscious State of Existence
The Schizophrenic State of Existence
The Dogmatic State of Existence
The Reasoned State of Existence
Something
Absolute
Physical
Known
Nothing
Demonic
Mental
Hallucinated
Spiritually
Hope
Mystical
Believed
Idea
Intellectual
Abstract
Proved
OBJECTIVE
EMOTIONAL
SUPERNATURAL
SCIENTIFIC
Sensed
Knowledge
Appearance
Aberration
Accepted
Faith
Created
Explained

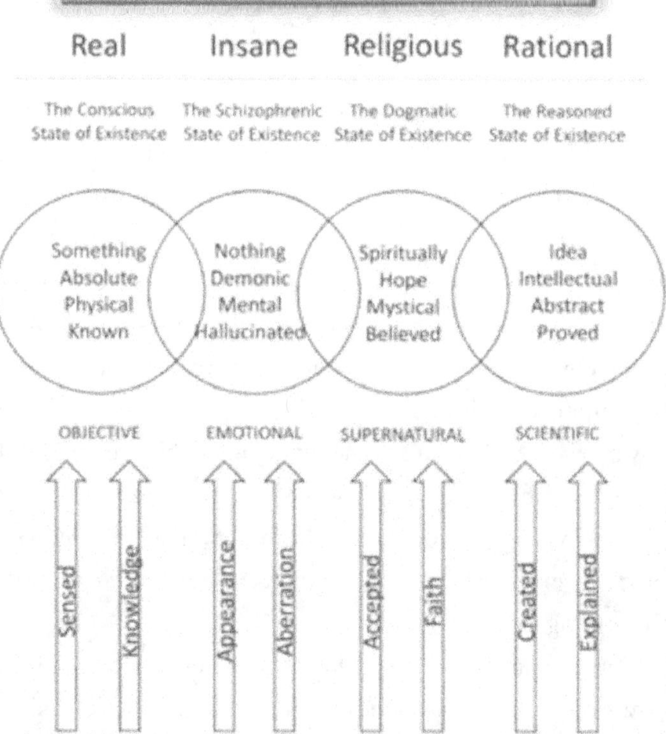

Every person who has ever lived, every person who now lives, and every person who will ever live at any time in the future can be found somewhere in the above "Human Nature" graphic.

This we all have in common. We all come into the world in the same way. We enter into an environment we have not experienced in the past. We have sensual responses to our new environment that we have not experienced in the past. We breathe air, but we have not breathed air before. We drink milk, but we have not drunk milk before. We hear babies cry, but we have not heard babies cry in the past. We smell flowers, but we have not smelled flowers before. We taste pureed spinach, but we have not tasted pureed spinach before. We become cold, but we have not been cold before. We become hungry, but we have not been hungry before. We feel the weight of our body, but we have not felt the weight of our body before.

We immediately enter into an environment that is foreign to us. This can be a very scary experience. We soon begin to realize we have a caregiver, that there is someone who is taking care of our needs, who is solving our problems. This caregiver makes us feel better when we begin to hunger. This caregiver makes us feel better when we begin to get cold. This caregiver is someone we begin to trust. We begin to depend on the wisdom of our caregiver. The very nature of our existence as a living being depends on this caregiver acting in a proper human manner.

We soon begin to release our fears and concerns to the loving attention of our caregiver. This allows us to concentrate on other things. We begin to concentrate on the nature of the environment in which we find ourselves, and our relationship to and within it.

However, when Aunt Emma rushes up to us laughing, crying, and yelling, "Oh, what a beautiful child," this can be very scary experience because it appears she is coming into our world from afar, as if from nowhere. Our sensual range is very short, and so it seems as if she is coming from nowhere and then returning to that same place.

As we mature, our senses mature along with us, and we begin to understand the real nature of Aunt Emma and the other things around her, including the real nature of our caregiver.

However, as we mature, and if our fears of the environment where we live are not abated, others may interpret this as a symptom of insanity or schizophrenia or some other serious mental illness. This is because maturing and remaining fearful of the environment within which one lives is not a normal mental condition.

We are dependent on our caregiver to resolve our fears, to solve fundamental problems for us, to support our survival needs and to instill happiness into our experience of our own physical person. We are dependent on our caregiver for everything, including our life and happiness.

Our relationship with our caregiver is of a godly nature. We implicitly trust the actions of our caregiver and faithfully accept the loving advice our caregiver offers us. We implicitly believe that the consequence of doing so will be compatible with our nature as a specific kind of being, a human being. We are (by our nature as a human being) believers in the goodness, kindness, wisdom, and intelligence of our caregiver.

As we mature and eventually separate ourselves from the godly attention of our caregiver, our need to be cared for and our need to have fundamental problems resolved does not magically go away. We look for another source. We look for persons whose advice we can trust and upon whose intellect we can depend on to solve the most fundamental problems facing human beings. We look for persons who seem to have all the answers we seek. This is how, and when, religion steps in to fill the void.

We remain under the influence of our chosen and trusted religious advisors, sometimes for a very long time. Sometimes the influence of our trusted religious advisors on our thinking, and thereby on our actions, never goes away. This is because we are busy doing other things. We do not have time to stop and think fundamentally. We find it much easier and less stressful to believe our trusted religious advisors have already done the thinking required for them to understand the nature of human nature and what its happy existence requires. And so, we accept their advice in the same way as we accepted the loving advice of our caregiver.

We are busy working at our job. We are busy taking care of our family. We are busy trying to solve real problems in the real world within which we find ourselves. We may be sick; the people we are dealing with may be mean. And so, we maintain our religious affiliations just because it is easier than the alternative: fundamental thinking.

Following in the path taken by countless others, believing in their beliefs, and accepting their advice seems to be much less troublesome than thinking on our own terms and solving our own problems, that is, by using our own intellect to discover the answers to the most fundamental of questions facing human beings.

It is not until we reach a more advanced state of existence, in which we have solved most of our day-to-day problems, that we finally have the time to just sit and think—fundamentally. To think about what we are, where we are living, and what the relationship between these two must be prior to being able to consider *ourselves* to be a properly functioning human being.

Only then can we begin to translate what we know into intelligence. Only then can we begin to conceptualize our sensually acquired knowledge into intelligence and then begin to explain what we are, where we are living, and what these say about how we must behave prior to being able to consider *ourselves* to be a properly functioning human being.

We eventually discover that to do this, we must fully remove ourselves from any influence our trusted religious advisors may have on our behavior and from their dependence on religious doctrine. Any hold religious doctrine maintains over our mind affects how well our mind is able to conceptualize what it knows to be the case into intelligence. Only then are we able to begin to explain the nature of human nature and that upon which its happy existence depends.

The remainder of this book will explain how that intellectual transformation can, does, and has occurred within the minds of people just like you. People who had also turned off their mind, people whose thinking and actions had also been determined for them by their trusted advisors (religious or otherwise). And, yes, it was a very scary transformation for them.

I understand and therefore can speak to the fear and emotional trauma accompanying such an enormous intellectual transformation to and within one's own mind.

For twenty years following the death of my daughter, I personally experienced it.

Recall when we discussed the three fundamental types of sound.

Chair

Recall when I said it is much easier to point and say "chair" than it is to explain why one uttered the sound visually symbolized in this manner: chair. For example, if this object at which I am pointing was not within the sensual range of the sense organs extending from your brain, I would need to explain why I uttered the sound visually symbolized in this manner—*chair*. And that requires a great deal of effort.

Water

Like *chair*, *water* is also called a word. *Chair* and *water* are called *words* because they directly designate or audio/visually denote the existence of the physical characteristics of an object in reality.

The meaning of the words *chair*, and *water* can be physically demonstrated. For example, when I point at this and utter the sound visually symbolized as *water*, my purpose for uttering it is sensually available to you. You do not have to think about it; you only have to know it. You automatically know why I uttered the sound visually symbolized as *water*.

Chair and *water*, in this way, are called *words*. Again, words directly designate or audio/visually denote the existence of the absolute nature of the physical characteristics of a real something.

Space

Space is rather different. Space does not designate or denote the existence of a physical object; it does not denote, and therefore intellectually "stand in the place of," the physical characteristics of a real something. Space is not a real something that can be walked up to and touched or pointed at. Therefore, *space* is called a *concept*. Concepts are derived from the understood existence of the abstract nature of perceptualized ideas, whereas words are derived from the sensually known existence of the absolute nature of the physical characteristics of the objects of reality.

Time

Time does not denote the physical characteristics of a real something. Time is not a word. Time is a concept, and concepts explain something about that which is known to be the case. Again, words *denote*, concepts *explain*.

Time is not real. Time is ideal. Time was created by the human mind in an effort to explain a specific aspect of the existence of the absolute nature of physical reality and how it functions. Time is not what it explains the existence of; time is simply an audio/visual symbol created to explain why the existence of its ideal nature exists. Time, then, explains a certain aspect of the abstract nature of intelligence rather than more simply denoting the existence of the absolute nature of an object in physical reality.

It is in this way that *time* is called a concept rather than a word. But notice the important linkage between words and concepts. Concepts are derivations of ideas abstracted from the existence of the absolute nature of physical reality. It is in this way that concepts are linked to reality; they are reality, explained.

Distance

Distance is also a concept. Distance explains something about the abstract nature of some aspect of the absolute nature of physical reality. All concepts have this in common. Concepts explain something that is understood to be the case about the absolute nature of the physical characteristics of the objects in reality, whereas words simply denote (or intellectually stand in the place of) the existence of the sensual influence of those same physical characteristics on a human brain. It is in this way that concepts are said to explain why ideas exist rather than more simply just physically denoting, i.e., pointing at with some kind of physical gesture, the existence of the objects upon which their ideal nature depends.

Universe

Universe does not denote the existence of a real physical something. That which *Universe* denotes the existence of does not exist in a sensually knowable way, it exists in a rationally understood way.

The idea explained by the definition of the concept *universe* is dependent on the absolute nature of physical reality for the explanation to be considered rational (that is, pertaining to reality). *Universe* is not what the existence of the absolute nature of physical reality is; it is what the abstract nature of an idea is. Universe, then, denotes the existence of an idea. The idea that is *universe* was created by the human mind to explain that physical reality does exist, and that it exists as a concept resulting from knowledge rather than from a hallucination, belief, or a lie.

"The existence of the absolute nature of the physical characteristics of reality" is not a word statement; it is a conceptual statement. This is because "the existence of the absolute nature of the physical characteristics of reality" does not denote a naturally existing real something (an object), but instead it explains the nature of a rationally created something, an idea.

Life

The issue is not "Does life exist?" or "What is life?" The issue is "Why does life exist?" This *life* is the existence of life. This **life** is life. **Life** is a creation of the human mind. Like all concepts, like all words, **life** is a creation of the human mind. The human mind is responsible for bring **life** into existence right here on earth. But why?

Why was life created? What is its purpose? What is its meaning? Why did the human mind create life and therefore must be held responsible bringing life into existence right here on earth?

Is *life* a word? Is *life* a concept? Perhaps *life* is both.

Note: Words denote the sensually known existence of the absolute nature of some aspect of physical reality. Since words are created to denote something that is sensually known to exist, and since the physical characteristics of life are not something that is sensually known to exist, then whatever its existence is, it must be explained.

This requirement—the requirement of explanation—would seem to require *life* to be considered a concept. But since *life* does have an absolute physical nature, and since concepts denote only the abstract nature of ideas, then *life* is not (it cannot be considered to be) a concept. *Life* must be considered to be a word.

But wait! The existence of the physical nature of life is not sensually known to exist! How, then, can it be considered a word? What aspect of the absolute nature of reality does *life*, the word, denote the sensually known physical characteristics of? What aspect of the absolute nature of human existence does *life* denote the sensually known physical characteristics of? What aspect of the absolute nature of the real physical world where you and I live does *life* denote the sensually known existence of?

Why Does Life Exist?

How is this dilemma to be resolved? It is resolved by creating a new type of concept, the purpose of which is to explain the absolute nature of that which the physical characteristics of is not or cannot be sensually known to exist. That is the concept of ***understand***.

Understanding the Physical Nature of Life

We can understand the physical nature of life by observing its influence on that which *is* sensually known to exist. This is done by observing that animate objects are physically different from inanimate objects. It is the sensually known existence of that physical difference that permits us to denote it with an audio/visual symbol called a *word*. And the word created to denote the existence of the physical difference existing between the animate and the inanimate is *life*. This is why the human mind created *life*. It exists only because the existence of the physical difference between the animate and the inanimate is sensually known to exist.

But notice that the word *life* does not explain what that difference is. That function is left to its definition. The word *life* denotes the existence of that physical difference, but its definition explains what that physical difference is. *Life* is a word, but its definition is conceptual.

Note the following and apply it whenever necessary: The term *life* is called a word because its audio/visually denotes the existence of the absolute nature of the physical characteristics of something that is "intellectually" understood to exist (as opposed to being sensually known to exist). Its definition is conceptual because it explains something about why the word *life* was created by the mind function of the human brain.

If those people who have purposefully blown themselves up, instead of believing that their trusted religious advisors were acting in their best interest, had thought about what the actual eternal nature of the consequence of their actions was going to be, would they have done that?

No—of course not! But now it is too late.

What advice would you have offered those same people if you had the opportunity to do so? What advice are you now giving to your own children and grandchildren?

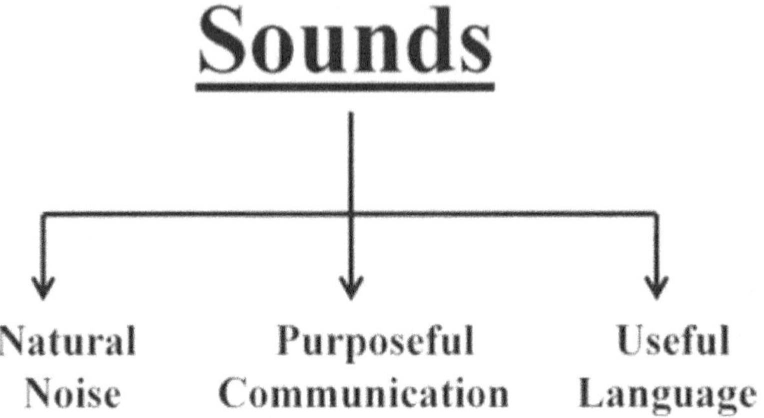

Recall when the three fundamental types of sound were being discussed.

Noise

Recall the discussion about the naturally occurring sounds of nature called *noise*. Noise occurs as a natural consequence of nature interacting with nature at the inanimate level. *Noise* is the audio/visual symbol created to denote the sensually known existence of the physical characteristics of naturally occurring sound.

Noise is not what the existence of the physical characteristics of naturally occurring sound is; it is merely the audio/visual symbol created to denote that its sensually known characteristics do physically exist. It is for this reason that *noise* is called a *word symbol*.

Communication

Also recall the discussion of purposefully created animal sound. The non-humans, the beasts, sensually know that the objects of nature do exist. They purposefully symbolize what is sensually known to exist in reality by making specific types of sound to denote the *existence* of its physical characteristics. Purposefully created animal sound is not called *noise*; it is called *communication*.

The purposefully created sounds of animal communication are not conceptual; they are not even called *words*. The reason for this is that they lack a defined meaning or understood purpose. The sounds of beastly animal communication are only symbolic. They only vocally symbolize the sensually known existence of real objects and their relationships.

Animal communication takes many forms. It symbolizes danger, anger, and a desire to mate. It symbolizes acceptance and submission. Do humans also communicate these kinds of things via sound symbols? Yes, they do! Humans are animals, after all!

However, at the human level of "beastly" communication, the sound symbols used to communicate what is sensually known to exist <u>are</u> called *words*. They are called words only because they include a definition. Words have a defined (conceptualized, true, accurate, verifiable, real) meaning and purpose. Again, beastly communication exists absent a defined meaning or purpose. Humans have a *defined* and therein an *understood* style of communication, while beasts have a *known* and therein only a *symbolic* style of communication.

The difference is enormous. It is the difference between knowing and understanding. It is the difference between revealing reality and revealing intelligence. It is the difference between existing properly and living happily. It is the difference between knowing that one exists and being able to explain why. It is the difference between beast and human, between acceptance and reason, between religion and intelligence.

Language

Also recall the discussion of purposefully created human sound. Humans purposefully make specific types of sound to explain something they understand about the nature of nature, including the nature of human nature. The sounds humans use to explain what is understood to be the case is not called *communication*, it is called *language*.

Whereas beasts make sounds to symbolically communicate what they sensually know to be the case, humans use language to explain what they understand about the nature of human nature and that upon which its happy existence depends.

The difference between the beastly irrational style of human communication and the intelligent use of human language is called *understanding*. Whereas beastly functioning humans base their conclusions on their instinctual emotional reactions to what is sensually known to exist, intelligent humans function based on what they understand about the existence of the absolute nature of physical reality, necessarily including the rational nature of human reality.

Humans are a specific kind of animal. They not only act purposefully in the sense that beasts act purposefully, but they also function intellectually. *Human* denotes the existence of the physical characteristics of the intellectual animal. In this usage of the term *human*, it is called a *word*, much like *dog* and *horse* are called words. But since its definition explains why the word *human* exists, it (the definition) is considered to be conceptual.

Under the idea visually symbolized as *language*, most of the terms used are conceptual. They are conceptual because they explain the abstract nature of reasoned ideas rather than, more simply, denoting the existence of the absolute nature of physical objects. Communication is reality symbolized; reality is symbolized with terms called words. Language is reality idealized; reality is idealized with terms called concepts. *Time*, *distance*, and *space* are examples of how reality has been idealized with concepts.

The non-human animals, the beasts, have not demonstrated the ability to idealize reality. They, therefore, cannot be considered to possess an intellect. Their sound symbols cannot be called either *words* or *concepts* because they do not have a defined, nor understood, reason for their existence. The best that can be said about beastly communication is that they use sounds to vocally symbolize the existence of that which their brain sensually knows to exist.

Notice how the language of the people we have hired to run our government for us seems to be a very noisy kind of human sound. This is because they seem to have abdicated their human intellect to a lesser standard. They have abdicated their reasoned intelligence in favor of altruistic belief. In other terms, they believe it is better to give favors than to create profit. Our hired hands see themselves as our caregivers, our parent, our protectors, our Aunt Emma. This is not the job they were hired to do. They were hired to function as our legal agents (our fictitious persons) only in those instances where we are not available to so act. Their actions are strictly controlled by the contract we hold with them, which they have taken a public oath to uphold.

Most of them need to be fired. We have done a lousy job of interviewing and hiring the right kinds of people to run our government for us. That being the kinds of people who actually do have an intellect equal to ours and are not afraid to use it in our best interest.

But this book is not about politics; it's about finding a physically based, purposefully reasoned, intellectually understandable explanation for the real existence of **God**, right here on earth.

As previously noted, like the non-human animals, the beasts, humans have the ability to create specific kinds of sound symbols to denote the existence of that which is sensually known to exist.

However, unlike the non-human animals, humans have the added ability to create specific kinds of visual symbols to denote the existence of the sound symbols they had previously created. *God* is an example of a visual symbol the human mind has created to denote the existence of a previously created sound symbol.

Was the visual symbol *God* created to denote something other than the vocally created sound symbol *God?* No, it was not!

Is the sound symbol *God* something other than what the visual symbol *God* was created to denote the vocalized existence of? No, it is not!

Then the issue is not "Does God exist?" nor is it "What is God?" The issue is "Why does God exist?"

God is an audio/visual symbol created by the human mind. The human mind is responsible for bringing God into existence right here on earth. But why?

What is God's purpose? What is God's meaning? What is God's application in a real physical word? We bring God into the sensual range of others by uttering its sound symbol and/or scribing its visual symbol. When we audio/visually bring God into existence, it is God that others hear and/or see.

<u>What do we tell others when they ask us to explain why we bring God into existence?</u>

Do we create God because we need to denote the existence of the absolute nature of the physical characteristics of a real something? In other terms, is *God* a *word?*

Do we create God in response to a need to explain something about the abstract nature of human intelligence? In other terms, is *God* a *concept*?

Do we create God to denote the mystical nature of nothing at all? In other terms, is *God* audio/visual evidence of the unknown and unknowable existence of some kind of religious deity, supernatural power, supreme intellect, or magical spirit?

Do we create God simply as a noise uttered for no known reason or understandable purpose? In other terms, is God evidence of *insanity*?

To proceed any further with this discussion, we must define the terms we use in a very specific way. The requirement is that the terms we use from this point forward be defined in such a way that they will apply to every person who has ever lived, to every person who now lives, and to every person who will ever live at any time in the future.

Absent such a rigorous requirement, the conclusions we reach will not be able to withstand the pressure of their own absurdity. The absence of such a requirement will leave open the door of human opinion, whim, crying, prayer, pleading, begging, force, threat, demand, and all like nonsense.

The universal nature of this requirement demands the development of a new philosophy. A philosophy based in the conceptual nature of human intelligence. A philosophy based on what is understood to be the case with regard to what we are, where we are living, and what these require of our physical, emotional, and intellectual behavior prior to being able to consider *ourselves* to be a properly functioning human being.

Defining the terms of a philosophy in such a manner will allow us to use them to explain the nature of human nature and that upon which its happy existence depends.

Such a philosophy has been created. I call it ***The Philosophy of Explanation***.

CHAPTER 5

The Science of Philosophy

The most useful and applicable philosophy developed to date is the *Philosophy of Objectivism*. Where it is based on the absolute nature of physical reality, ***The Philosophy of Explanation*** is based on the abstract nature of human intelligence (the only kind!).

The Philosophy of Explanation is a natural result of the purposeful transformation of the metaphysical basis of reality into the epistemological basis of intelligence. As such, ***The Philosophy of Explanation*** is not different from The Philosophy of *Objectivism*; it is its epistemological advancement. The intellectual basis of ***The Philosophy of Explanation*** is more useful for explaining the rational nature of human nature than what the metaphysical basis of *The Philosophy of Objectivism* allows it to be considered.

Those who loathe the physical approach to explaining the rational nature of human nature offered by The Philosophy of Objectivism may find the intellectual approach offered by ***The Philosophy of Explanation*** more to their liking.

Unlike The Philosophy of Objectivism, ***The Philosophy of Explanation*** is able to address the most fundamental questions facing man, such as "Why do life, time, space, distance, universe, human, happiness, eternity, and (of course) God exist?"

As the beginning point for the development of ***The Philosophy of Explanation***, and as the fundamental philosophical foundation for the development of ***The Philosophy of Explanation***, I will first present several edited definitions of what the science of philosophy is, as that is explained by Ayn Rand during her creation of The Philosophy of Objectivism.

══════════════════

THE SCIENCE OF PHILOSOPHY

Following are edited excerpts of Ayn Rand's writings:

1) Your actions are a consequence of your philosophy. Their result on your person is not; this is left to the laws of nature. As a human being, you have no choice about your need of philosophy. Your only choice,

in this regard, is whether you define the parameters of your philosophy or whether you blindly follow another's.

2) Philosophy deals with those aspects of the universe that pertain to everything that exists. Philosophy is the foundation of science, the selector of man's values and goals, the organizer of man's thoughts and thereby his actions.

3) Philosophy is that science which studies the nature of existence, of man, and of man's relationship to existence. The fundamental branches of philosophy are *metaphysics* and *epistemology*. It is on the basis of a knowable universe (metaphysics) and one's rational grasp of it (epistemology) that one can define the secondary branches of philosophy: ethics, morality, and esthetics.

4) The task of philosophy is to provide man with a comprehensive view of what it means to act properly. In order to evaluate a given philosophical premise, ask what—if applied—it would do to human life, beginning with your own. This view will serve as a base, a frame of reference, for your actions. This view will give you the nature of the universe with which you must deal (metaphysics), and the means by which to deal with it (epistemology). It will provide the standard by which you choose your goals and values in regard to your life and your character (ethics), and in regard to your relationship with others (morality). Your means of explaining this view is *esthetics*.

5) In order to live, man must act; in order to act, man must make choices; in order to make choices, man must define a code of values; in order to define a code of values, man must discover the nature of his existence as the rational being. Since man knows what he is and where he lives, his only task is to understand how these define how he must behave prior to being considered a properly functioning human being. Man needs philosophy.

From these philosophical premises, it is possible to develop a new philosophy, a philosophy capable of answering the most fundamental questions facing human beings, such as "Why does God exist?"

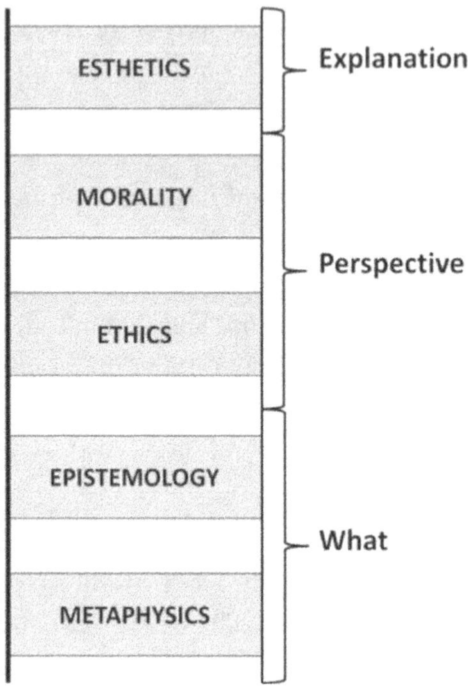

The above accompanying graphic illustrates the structure of a properly constructed philosophical ladder. Any properly organized philosophy is constructed in this hierarchical manner. A properly constructed philosophical ladder will consist of these five steps or rungs. These are then divided into three sub-groups or areas of concentrated interest.

1. **The What Group:** What is it that we are interested in discussing?
    a. Are we interested in knowing? Which is metaphysics.
    b. Are we interested in understanding? Which is epistemology.

2. **The Perspective Group:** From what point of view are we interested in discussing metaphysics and epistemology?

a. Are we interested in discussing them from an ethical point of view?
    Which is personal.
b. Are we interested in discussing them from a moral point of view?
    Which is social.

3. **The Explanation Group:** What method will we use to explain what
    we have learned? Which is esthetics. Will we use:
    a. Language
    b. Art
    c. Sculpture
    d. Architecture
    e. Dance or some other?

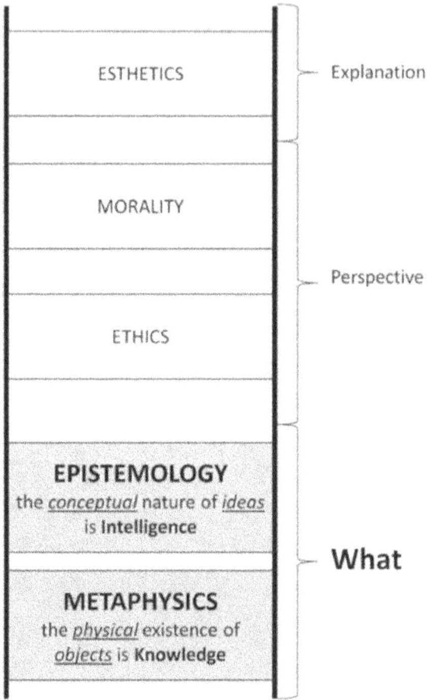

When considering "The What Group" of the philosophical ladder, the focus of our interest is "What is it that we are interested in discussing?"

1. Are we interested in:
    a. Knowing that physical objects exist? Which is metaphysics.
    b. Understanding the conceptual nature of intelligence? Which is epistemology.
2. Are we interested in:
    a. Knowledge? Which is metaphysics.
    b. Intelligence? Which is epistemology.

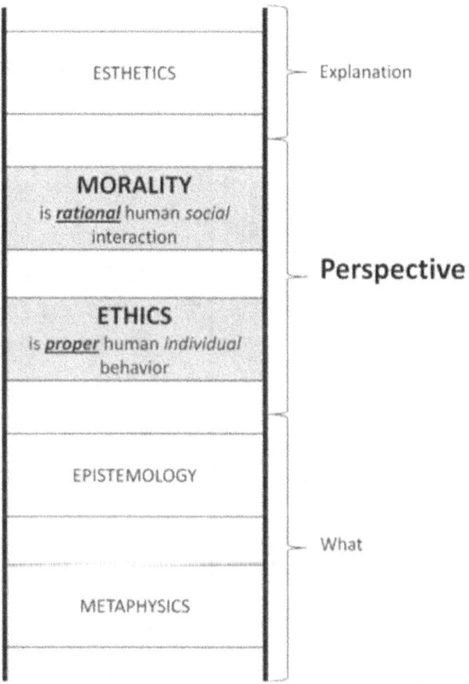

When considering "The Perspective Group" of the philosophical ladder, the focus of our interest is "From what perspective, from what point of view, are we interested in discussing metaphysics and epistemology?"

1. Are we interested in discussing them from:
    a. A personal point of view? Which is ethics.
    b. A social point of view? Which is morality.

2. Are we interested in understanding:
    a. What proper human individual behavior is? Which is ethics.
    b. What rational social interaction is? Which is morality.

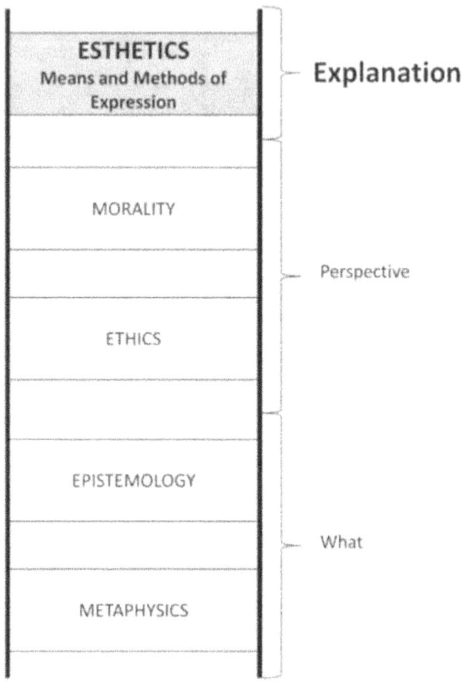

When considering the final rung of the philosophical ladder, "The Explanation Group," the focus of our interest is on being able to explain the nature of human nature, necessarily including that upon which its happy existence depends.

1. Truth
   a. Our interest here is in explaining the truth about the intellectual nature of human beings, and in doing so explaining the rational nature of the God of human nature.

Note that this is a ladder, a philosophical ladder. It is, therefore, impossible to explain the true nature of happiness until we fully advance up the philosophical ladder from the bottom to the top.

All of our esthetical premises must first begin from a sound philosophical basis in metaphysics; only then can these be advanced to a sound philosophical basis in epistemology, and only then can these be advanced to a sound philosophical basis in ethics, and only then can these be advanced to a sound philosophical basis in morality.

It is not until we have fully advanced to the top of the philosophical ladder that we can stand firmly on the esthetical rung and, from there, explain the true nature of human nature and that upon which its continued happy existence depends.

As previously stated, in order to do this, we must begin at the bottom of the philosophical ladder and work our way to the top. We must then begin with "The What Group."

CHAPTER 6

Discussing "The What Group"

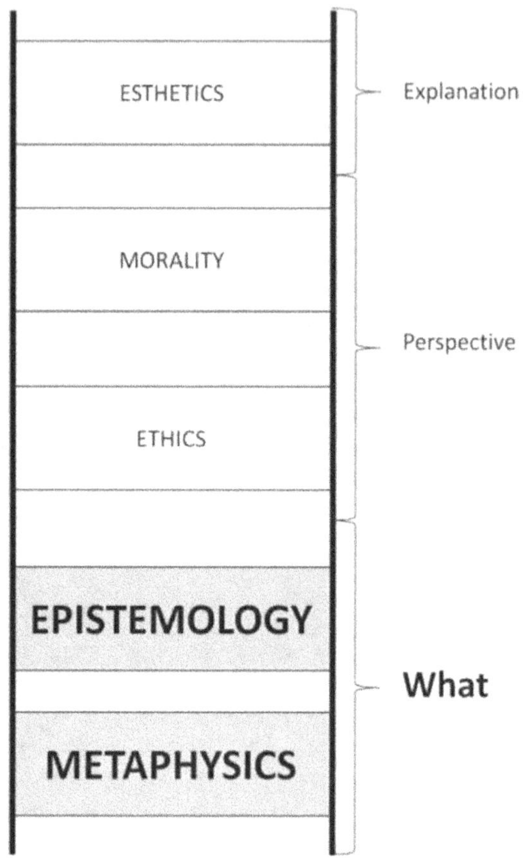

Under "The What Group," our interest is in differentiating:

METAPHYSICS		EPISTEMOLOGY
Words	from	Concepts
Knowledge	from	Intelligence
Communication	from	Language

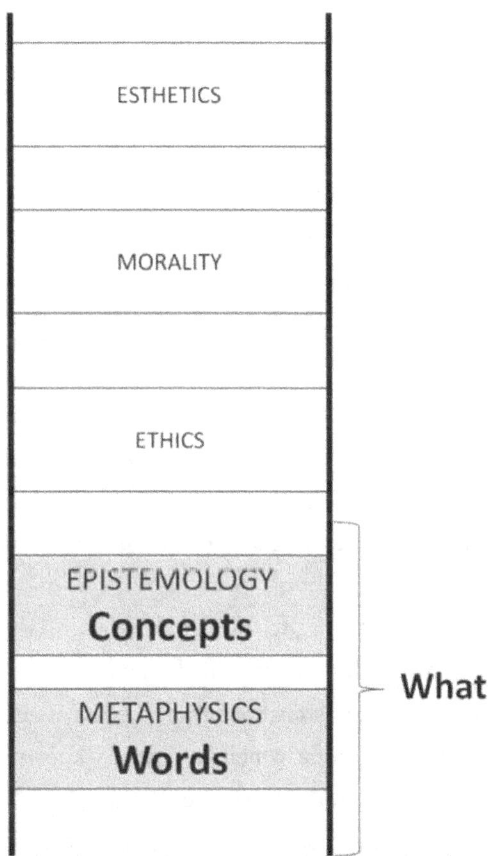

The Metaphysics of Words

When considering how to explain the metaphysical rung of the philosophical ladder, the focus of our concern is on the *existence* of the absolute nature of the physical characteristics of the objects of reality.

The existence of the physical characteristics of objects in reality is absolute. This is not to say that things in reality do not change, they do. However, their *existence* is not a time-sensitive idea.

When we say things exist absolutely, we are saying:

a. They are what they are,

b. They are not that which they are not,

c. They do not exist in some kind of intermediate state between what they are and what they are not.

These are the three laws of logic:

a. The law of identity

b. The law of non-contradiction

c. The law of excluded middle

The *existence* of that which is "sensually" known to exist is denoted by the use of terms called words. Words are audio/visual symbols created based on what is sensually known to exist in a physically absolute manner. Importantly, the word *created* is not the same thing as the real thing it was created to denote the sensually known **existence** of. It is merely an audio/visual symbol purposefully created to denote (i.e., to stand in the place of) the absolute nature of the existence of that real thing's physical characteristics.

A word permits us to transmit, and thereby place within the brain of another, symbolic evidence of that which is sensually known to exist in a real physical way. It is of particular interest to note that purposefully created human sound symbols can be transferred into the brains of certain non-humans. A dog, for example, can be trained to respond to the human sound visually symbolized as *sit*. It is also of particular interest to note that the reverse has never occurred. There is not even one instance where a non-human (a beast) has trained, or has ever attempted to train, or has ever demonstrated a desire to train, a human to respond to its sound symbols. And yet, animals have been observed to communicate with others of their own species. The reason is clear and will soon be explained.

The Epistemology of Concepts

As previously noted, it is not until we become properly founded on the metaphysical rung of philosophy that we are prepared to advance to the epistemological rung.

Having now become metaphysically proficient, we are ready to become epistemologically proficient.

To avoid becoming confused about what it is we are talking about, whenever we change the focus of our discussion from one rung of the philosophical ladder to the next, we must change the terms we use.

Each rung of the philosophical ladder has its own unique set of terms. For example, metaphysical terms are called *words*, whereas epistemological terms are called *concepts*. Ethical terms are considered to be personal, where moral terms are considered to be social. Esthetics is the application and use of the terms previously created to form a reason-based explanation.

Recall that under metaphysics we are using terms called words. Under metaphysics, our interest is on the sensually known existence of the absolute nature of the physical characteristics of objects. In other terms, under metaphysics, we speak about that which is sensually known to exist or that which can be sensually known to exist. The means of knowing that an object exists is brain-sensing. The human brain has five sense organs extending from it. It is the sense organs of the human brain that form a naturally occurring physiological and electrochemical "interference" relationship with the other objects of physical reality. It is in this way that the **existence** of the absolute nature of physical characteristics of an object is electrochemically transmitted via nerves into the rest of the brain for further processing by its automatically occurring consciousness function.

On the other hand, when we speak epistemologically, we are using terms called *concepts*. Concepts reveal intelligence as opposed to revealing what is sensually known to be the case. Concepts are derived from ideas, and ideas are based on what is understood to be the case about that which is sensually known to be the case. The means of knowing *that* reality exists is *sensual*; the means of understanding its nature is *reason*.

When we apply our reason to understand, and from there to explain, the true nature of a real something or relationship, the result is a term called a *concept*. Concepts do not denote the physical nature of *reality*; they denote the reasoned nature of *intelligence*. The critical issue is not in knowing whether an idealized creation (a concept) exists but is in understanding *why* it was created.

Because ideas are creations of the human mind, they do not make sense, they can't make sense. This is because what they explain the existence of does not exist in a sensually knowable physical manner. Only physical objects can make sense. This is saying that it is only the **existence** of the absolute nature of the physical characteristics of an object that can cause a physiological and electrochemical interference, i.e., a sensual response, to occur to and within a brain.

Repeating, ideas do not exist in reality as objects; they exist in intelligence as terms called concepts. The source of the material from which the human mind creates its ideas is provided to it by the five sense organs extending from its brain. Recall that the existence of the actively occurring sensual influence of a real object on a brain is called **its** fact, i.e., the sensual influence exists "factually."

Under metaphysics, the sensually known existence of the physical entities of reality, called objects, is *absolute*. However: Under epistemology, the rationally understood existence of the mental entities of intelligence, called terms, is *abstract*. An abstract existent is that which has been abstracted from a something, the sensual existence of which, is factually known to exist by the mind function of a "human" brain.

Terms called words "point at" objects, whereas terms called concepts "explain" their nature.

To provide an explanation as to why a word was created only requires pointing at that which is responsible for it. This is called an *ostensive definition* or a definition by direct physical referencing. For example, when I point at this object and utter the sound visually symbolized as *chair*, you sensually know why I created that sound. You do not need to understand what the existence of its intellectual nature **means**; you only need to sensually know that the existence of its physical characteristics does *in fact* exist.

To explain the abstract meaning of a concept is a much more difficult task. This requires applying the preexisting conceptual content of one's mind to that task. The nature of the term *concept* itself is conceptual. Meaning that one's reason for creating the term concept *itself* must be explained; i.e., the reason for doing so can only be understood.

To explain why a conceptual term exists requires uttering and/or scribing the conceptual content of one's mind back into reality. This does require one to purposefully apply the reasoning power of one's mind to that task. The purpose driven application of the power of reason is called thinking. Thinking is the virtue of reason. It is thinking that results in one's conceptual content. But what do we think about? We think about that which we have stored within our mind as terms and their definitions. The purpose of thinking is to understand, and from there to explain the _origination_ of the terms one has stored within one's mind for future use and application. If a term is discovered to have been simply **accepted** into one's mind absent a sensually known source, and therefore absent an understandable reason, and therefore absent one's ability to explain why it exists, then, it (the term) must be discarded. To simply accept another's ideas as one's own is to not think about, or to not care about, what the naturally occurring consequences upon one's mind **will** be. To not think about, i.e., to not care about, the consequences resulting from one's behavior is to either hallucinate (the nonvolitional virtue of mental insanity), believe (the volitional religious virtue of unconditional acceptance), or lie (the evil virtue of purposeful deception). Perhaps it involves a little of each.

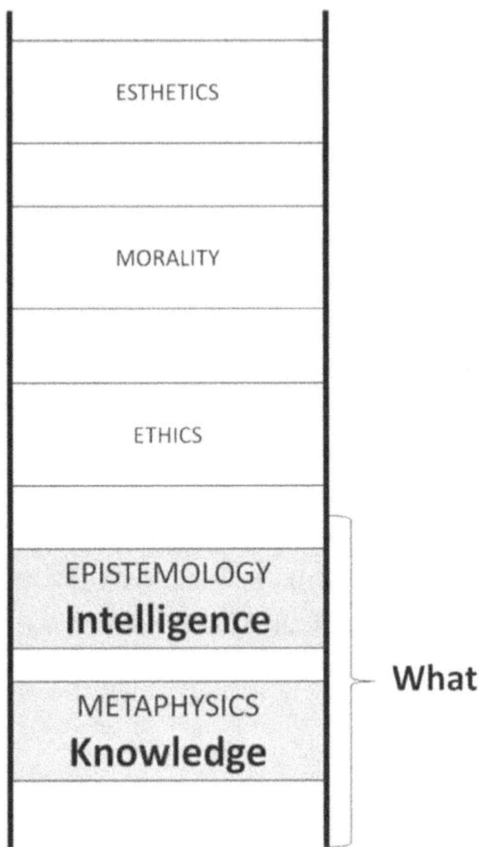

The Metaphysics of Knowledge

Again, on the metaphysical rung of The What Group, the focus of our interest is, what is knowledge? Recall: The source of knowledge is not what the objects of reality are; it is what the absolute nature of their *existence* is.

We purposefully direct the sense organs extending from our brain, enabling them to know <u>*that*</u> the objects of reality exist. However, the sense organs extending from our brain have a finite sensual range. This is saying that the human brain's sense organs cannot sensually know all that is available to be known about even one object. But they do know all that is available to be known that does fall within their sensual range.

Since a brain is not and therefore cannot be sensually stimulated by all the physical characteristics available to it from even one object, then, it is not proper to claim that a brain can sensually acquire all of the sources of knowledge available to it.

To solve this dilemma, we need to have a term specifically created to denote the existence of only that aspect of the absolute nature of the existence of the physical characteristics of reality that is sensually known to exist. That term is *data*. Data is that aspect of, or subset of, the existence of the absolute nature of the physical characteristics of an object falling within the sensual range of the sense organs extending from a human brain.

As we purposefully direct the sense organs extending from our brain to observe an object in reality, they (the sense organs) transmit the data which is automatically "sensually" known to exist back into our brain via nerves for further processing into the perceptual nature of knowledge. It is the information of which knowledge consists of that is abstracted from it to be conceptualized into intelligence.

When a scientist, doctor, engineer, student, parent, infant, or other is collecting data with which to draw a conclusion, make a decision, offer a recommendation, or to simply know that a something exists, that individual's brain is automatically collecting data about what the existence of the absolute nature of physical reality is.

"Knowing is that automatically occurring sensual event taking place between two objects when at least one of these objects is a brain." In other terms, the sensual acquisition of the source of data (a subset of the source of knowledge) is not optional. It is an innate aspect of how all animal brains operate and function, including the human brain.

To evaluate the veracity of this claim, simply look at an object. Now, without doing anything else, do not see it. You now understand what the automatically occurring data acquisition function of the sense organs extending from your brain is. You may not understand how it functions, but you do know that it is functioning and that you do not have, and cannot have, any influence over that. Data acquisition by a brain occurs automatically, and continuously.

The Epistemology of Intelligence

Again, when considering the epistemological rung of The What Group, the focus of our interest is intelligence.

Note here that epistemology is a step up on the philosophical ladder from metaphysics. It is proper to say that the epistemological nature of intelligence represents an evolutionary advancement over the metaphysical nature of the source of knowledge upon which its conceptual nature depends. In other terms, knowledge is the **existence** of the absolute nature of the physical characteristics of real objects… imaged, whereas intelligence is the **existence** of the information abstracted from knowledge…conceptualized.

Intelligence, then, is completely dependent on the *understood* existence of (not the sensually known existence of) the absolute nature of those sources of data which is sensually known to fall within the sensual range of the human brain. To exist metaphysically is to exist as a sensually knowable physical absolute. To exist epistemologically is to exist as a rationally understood conceptual abstraction.

The creative process responsible for abstracting information from knowledge, with which to conceptualize intelligence, is *reason*. Reason is the virtue of conceptualization and thinking is the virtue of reason. Intelligence is the epistemological concomitant of the absolute nature of the source of the knowledge upon which its conceptual nature depends. It is impossible to be considered intelligent in the absence of sensually knowing what it is one is talking about.

Note here that the term *concept* is the epistemological concomitant of the metaphysical term *object*. Like the epistemological term *intelligence* represents an evolutionary advancement over the metaphysical term *reality*, so does the epistemological term *concept* represent an evolutionary advancement over the metaphysical term *object*.

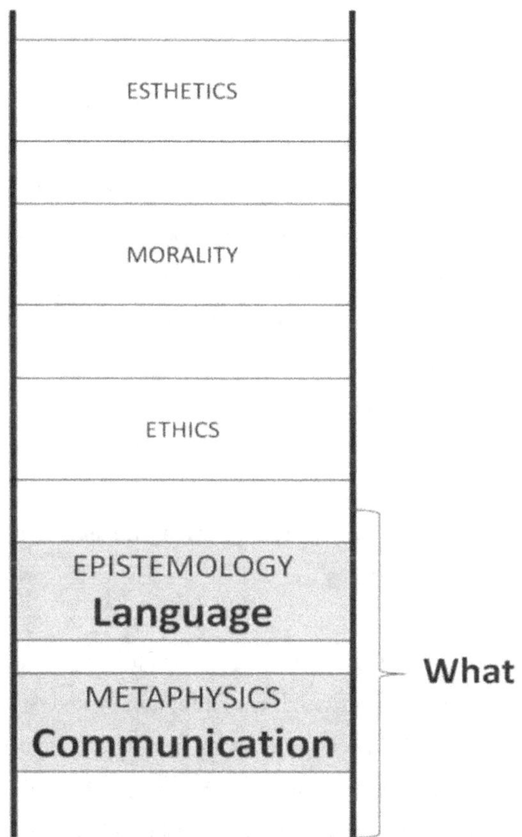

The Metaphysics of Communication

We transmit what is sensually known to exist into the brain of another by creating specific kinds of audio/visual symbols called *words*. Note that under the idea of communication, we do not transmit what we understand about what we know, we only transmit what is sensually known to exist. It is as if the word symbol and the object responsible for its creation are one and the same. Caution: They are not! An example: Water is not physical, it is intellectual. However, the something responsible for is creation is not intellectual, it exists as a sensually knowable physical absolute.

The Epistemology of Language

Under epistemology, we create audio/visual symbols called *concepts* to denote what is rationally understood about that which is sensually known to be the case. Concepts are used to explain how human's must and do interface with the objects of physical reality; necessarily including other humans in order to selfishly benefit from that experience (whether physical, emotional, or intellectual).

An intellectual term (called a concept) is vastly different from an emotional term (called a word); it is its epistemological expansion. The intellectual nature of *concepts* represents an evolutionary advancement over the emotional nature of *words*. *Concept* extends the emotional nature of *word* from sensual knowing into reasoned understanding. Where words are based in and therefore reveal reality, concepts are based in and therefore reveal intelligence. Intelligence, then, is the absolute nature of reality understood, i.e., conceptualized.

To exist physically is to be the source of the knowledge to explain why. To exist conceptually is to be the source of terms necessary to formulate an *irrefutable* explanation. When we use words, we reveal the absolute nature of objects, and we are externally focused. When we use concepts we reveal the abstract nature of intelligence, and we are internally focused. When we use concepts, we are explaining that which we understand to be the case about that which we sensually know to be the case with regard to our relationship with the other objects found in the physical environment where we live.

Note: An explanation has neither physical nor time constants. An explanation cannot be found in reality, no matter how long one looks for one there. Meaning that an explanation is rational rather than emotional, i.e., reasoned rather than accepted, i.e., intellectual rather than religious, i.e., conceptual rather than dogmatic, i.e., good rather than evil i.e., understood rather than believed.

As Promised

The reason none of the beasts (the non-human animals) have ever taught us their language or have never even demonstrated an interest in doing so is because beasts do not have a language. And this is because they do not have, have never demonstrated the existence of a perceptual mind, an understanding mind, a rational mind, a reasoning mind, a conceptual mind. They have not demonstrated that mental activity termed *conceptual-reasoning*. Meaning, they are not able to purposefully translate fact-based knowledge into conceptual intelligence. And it is the ability to conceptualize knowledge into intelligence that is a prerequisite for the creation of language. Language is evolutionarily different from what communication is, it is an epistemological expansion on the metaphysical nature of communication. Human language represents an evolutionary advancement over the metaphysical nature of beastly based human communication.

YES! Fundamentally speaking, humans are beasts. Beastly behaving humans run for public office and insidiously create laws to control the behavior of other humans. For example, the Sherman Anti-Trust Act. Intellectually behaving humans form reason-based relationships resulting in achievements. For example, Marriages, private agreements, and public corporations.

In the following pages we are going to examine the terms used within the ethics and morality rungs of the perspective group of *The Philosophy of Explanation*. The purpose is to eventually explain the true nature of human happiness and that upon which its continued existence depends.

This will likely proceed in a manner you have not experienced in the past. It is this author's seriously considered view that the existing manifold volumes of the philosophical works of countless others, covering many hundreds of years and written by those who are/were considered experts in the field of philosophic investigation, is not only grossly inaccurate and very misguided but may represent some kind of special, as yet undiagnosed, mental illness.

Then, in the remaining pages, I will reveal the real cause of the term "God."

CHAPTER 7

Discussing "The Perspective Group"

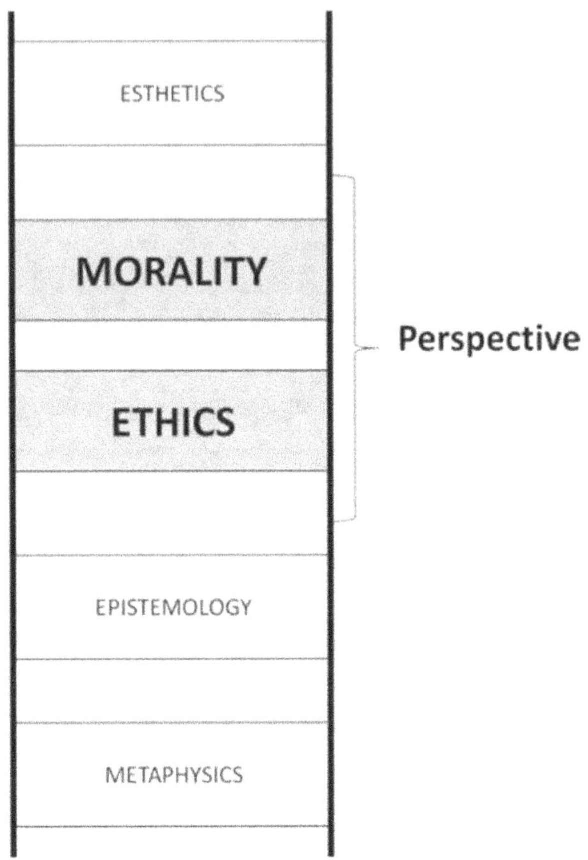

Under "The Perspective Group," our interest is in differentiating:

ETHICS		MORALITY
The Real	from	The Ideal
Individual	from	Society
Benefit	from	Profit
Selfishness	from	Capitalism
Natural Law	from	Contractual Law
Survival	from	Happiness

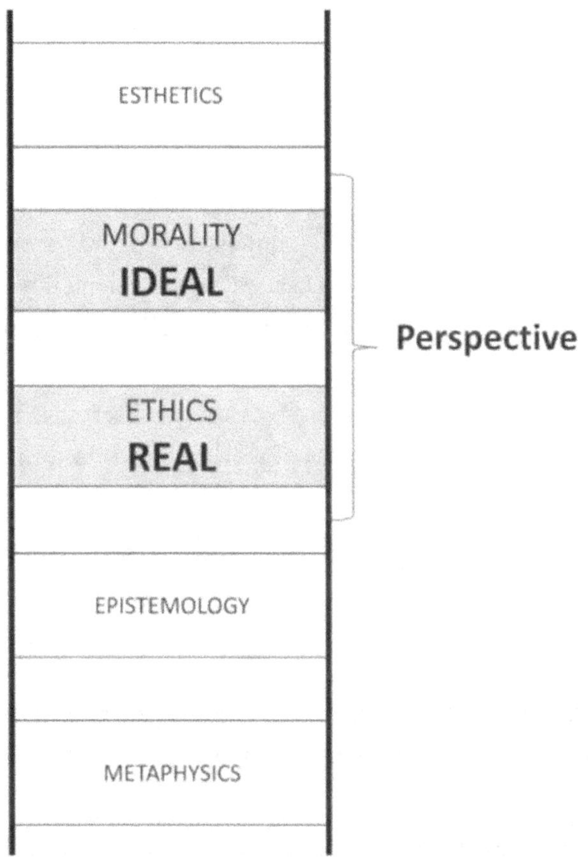

As previously noted, as the focus of our interest changes from one rung of the philosophical ladder to another, we must also change the terms we use. Since we are now moving from "The What Group" of philosophy to "The Perspective Group," we must change the terms we use; otherwise, others will become confused as to what it is we are talking about.

We note that The Perspective Group of philosophy is higher on the philosophical ladder than The What Group is. Since we have advanced above the epistemological rung of the philosophical ladder, the terms we use from here forward are primarily conceptual in nature. They are governed by the law of intelligence, which specifies that when we speak epistemologically, we are referencing the rational nature of human intelligence rather than the physical nature of objects.

When considering The Perspective Group of the philosophical ladder, the focus of our interest is from what perspective or from what point of view are we discussing metaphysical absolutes and epistemological abstractions? Are we discussing them from an ethical point of view? Or are we discussing them from a moral point of view?

It is important—even critically important—to point out that The Perspective Group is merely a highly focused "epistemological" view back into what The What Group consists of. In other terms, The Perspective Group is the intellectual concomitant of a specific aspect of The What Group.

In The Perspective Group the focus of our interest is the ethics of individual behavior and the morality of social interactions, whereas in The What Group our focus was on the absolute nature of the physical characteristics of objects (metaphysics) and the means of understanding what that is (epistemology).

The Ethics of the Real

Where *metaphysics* deals with the reality of all physical objects, *ethics* deals with the reality of a single physical object, the human being.

The Morality of the Ideal

Where *epistemology* deals with the reasoned nature of all ideas, *morality* deals with the reasoned nature of a single idea, the idea of society.

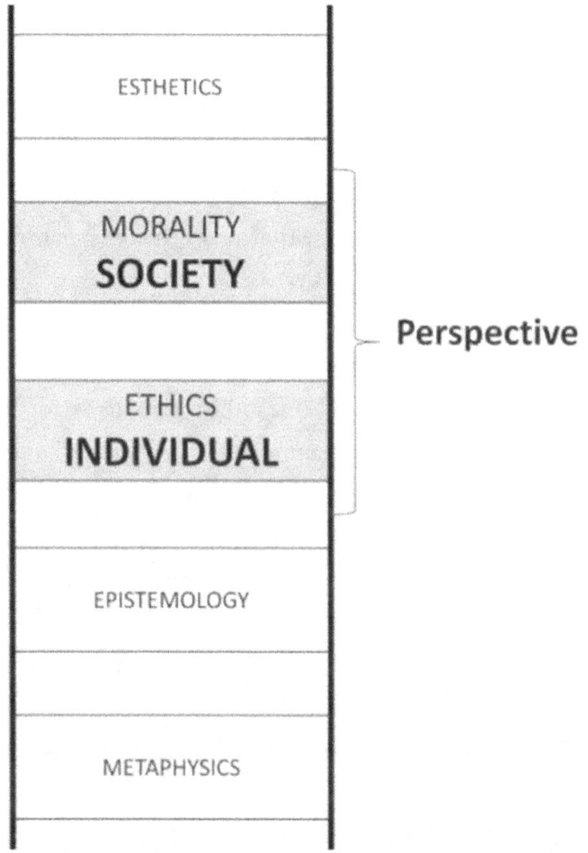

The Ethics of Individual Behavior

Under ethics, it is as if we are considering a person who is living on a deserted island all by himself. This person must function in a specific manner; he must function as a human being. This person cannot continue to exist on that island if he tries to function as a whale, an eagle, or a rosebush. His only alternative, his only option is to function as a human being.

Under ethics, a human is an individual object of physical reality. This requires that the terms we use be determined by the law of words, which states, "When we speak ethically, we speak about that which we sensually know to be the case."

But as previously stated, since we have advanced above the metaphysical rung of the philosophical ladder, the terms we use need to be determined by the law of concepts, which states, "When we speak epistemologically, we speak with regard to what we rationally understand is the case."

To act ethically is to behave in a properly functioning human manner. This requires one to think about the consequences of one's behavior and then only do that which will have a beneficial effect on one's person. To behave ethically is to "understand" what the nature of the consequences resulting from one's actions upon oneself will be.

The Morality of Social Interactions

Under morality we talk about a single idea, the idea of *society*. When we move our discussion from the ethics rung up to the moral rung, the rules defining proper human behavior are *expanded*. Under morality, the rules of behavior are no longer only determined by what constitutes purpose driven individual behavior; they are *additionally* determined by what constitutes reason driven **social interactions** between ethically behaving individuals. Therefore, under morality the number of terms available to formulate an expression is greater than under ethics.

But notice that *society* is a concept. Concepts denote ideas; they do not denote the absolute nature of physical reality. A "society," then, is not a real physical something. Meaning that society is an abstract ideal something. Society does not exist in an absolute sensually knowable way. It exists in an abstract intellectually understood way. It is not possible to describe a society using the same terms used to describe the individuals of which it consists of. This is why when discussing morality, the additional terms required for that purpose must be created.

Society is purely an idea. An idea derived from that which is sensually known to be the case is a rational idea. It is considered rational because it explains what society is and how individual humans are related to it. In a rational functioning society, the individuals of whom it consists of are behaving ethically. In other terms, while socially engaged, they are still acting in accordance with the laws of nature governing what human survival consists of and requires from their behavior right here on earth. It is the laws of nature determining the behavior of ethical functioning individuals that, when translated into a reason-based social interaction, determine how those same ethical functioning individuals behave when socially engaged; they behave morally.

The Laws of Man

It is the laws of nature governing proper human behavior that determine the laws reason-driven persons create when socially engaged. These are the laws of a rational functioning society. The laws of society, when governed by the laws of nature, are called ***moral laws***. They are called moral laws because they describe the behavior of ethical functioning human beings when those same human beings are socially engaged. Moral laws do not prescribe or dictate what constitutes proper individual behavior in a social setting; they only describe what it is.

To describe proper human behavior in a social setting, it must be observed. The consequences resulting naturally from the interactions occurring between individuals determine whether the behavior of those individuals is rational, whether or not those actions were determined by applying reason to understanding the fundamental purpose of human behavior, with that purpose being to remain in existence as a certain kind of organism…the human one!

The consequence must not conflict with the living nature of the individuals performing those actions. Further, it must not conflict with the living nature of any human now living or who will live at any time in the future, anywhere in the entire physical universe.

It is only in a moral-functioning society that we find properly behaving individuals, that is, ethically guided individuals. We do not find moral behaving individuals in any type of society the laws of which are detrimental to the ethical nature of properly functioning human beings.

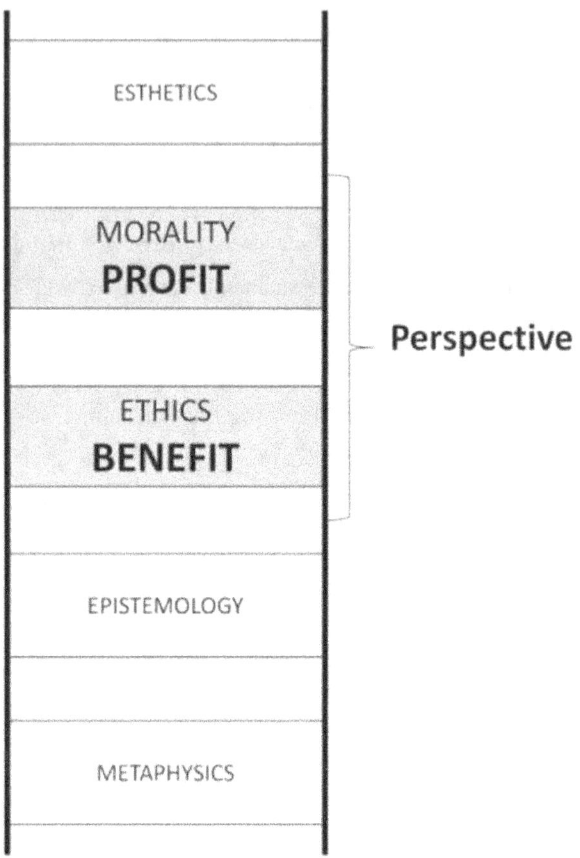

The Ethics of Benefit

Under ethics, individual action is considered proper only when the individual performing the action benefits from the naturally resulting consequence. Otherwise, that individual suffers by having created a consequence that is detrimental to his living person.

Ethics requires that the living existence of each individual person benefit from the naturally occurring consequence of his own actions. Again, ethics demands that the individual performing those actions benefit from them.

Consider the individual living alone on a deserted island. This person must perform specific actions; otherwise, his living person is going to suffer from not doing so. This is saying that the consequence is considered beneficial only if it satisfies a *survival* need of his living person.

The Morality of Profit

A social action is considered moral only when *both* individuals involved in that action are ethical actors. That each is functioning in a proper human manner, meaning that the primary goal of each is to benefit from his own actions. Only then can he engage another individual morally, i.e., only then can he engage another individual in a social interaction that is *profitable*.

We note that two properly functioning persons, two ethical actors, voluntarily working together, create a greater benefit for *themselves* than if each had individually performed those same actions. That "greater benefit" resulting naturally from their volitional social interaction is called *profit*. A moral interaction produces personal benefits in excess of what the individuals involved require. It is the **existence** of the excessive benefits produced that is re-termed into *profit*.

Proper individual action is considered ethical, and ethical action results in producing a beneficial consequence for the actor. Proper individual action, performed in a social setting, is considered rational, i.e., a reason-based social interaction. And the naturally occurring consequence of a reason-based social interaction produces a greater benefit for each of its participants. To avoid confusion, that <u>greater</u> benefit produced is renamed from benefit into *profit*.

Ethical functioning individuals profit from willingly engaging other ethical functioning individuals. Again and again, *profit* is merely the greater benefit realized when two ethical functioning individuals purposefully engage one another to their mutual benefit. A rational interaction, then, is that mutually agreed-to social interaction the purpose of which is to create a greater benefit for each participant. Again, each participant *must* benefit **to a greater extent** (i.e., excessively) from his jointly agreed-to interactions.

Socially produced profit, then, is the epistemological concomitant of the metaphysical nature of selfishly produced personal benefits. When the individuals of a society profit from their selfishly motivated interactions with other equally motivated individuals, those individuals are said to be *excessively* benefiting from those interactions. Importantly, each individual must understand, and agree, that the other must also benefit from their voluntary interaction with oneself. Each must not only agree that the other must benefit from their voluntary actions, but each must also "insist" on that being the case. Each must benefit but only in accordance with their contribution resulting in the production of a specific specified amount of the profitable outcome.

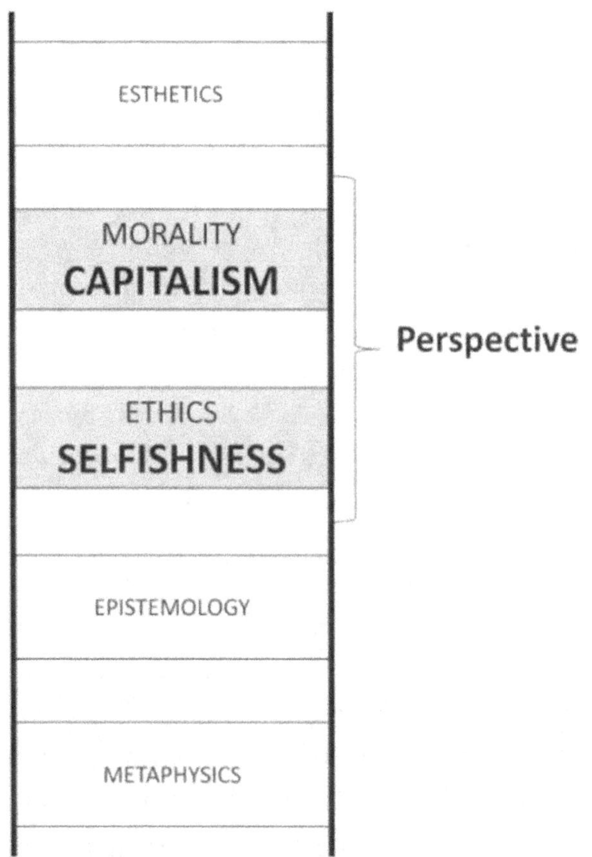

The Ethics of Selfishness

Beneficial action is selfish action. This is the principle of selfishness. The individual living alone on the deserted island must benefit from his actions. He has no other choice or option. His only interest is himself. His only interest is his continued existence as a living person on that island.

There is no other person on this island for him to be concerned about. His self-interest is his greatest and highest goal. This is the principle of *selfishness*. The principle of selfishness does not involve any other individual. There is no other person living on this island with this individual who is living there in a proper, selfishly motivated, human manner.

The consequences of his actions are not influencing, either positively or negatively, the existence of any other human being. He must, and does, act alone. He simply has no other option. He is, therefore, considered both a selfishly motivated and an ethically guided person. Meaning he is and must continue be a properly functioning, i.e., ethically guided, i.e., a selfishly motivated, human being in order to remain alive on that island.

The Morality of Capitalism

When translating the naturally occurring ethical principles of *individual selfishness* into the principles describing rational social interactions, we get the moral principles described by the idea of *capitalism*.

Where individually produced benefit is considered a proper consequence of selfishly motivated individual action, the social production of profit is considered to be a rational, or reason-based, consequence of capitalistically motivated social interactions.

The underlying moral premise governing the actions of selfishly motivated individuals when socially engaged is that they agree to engage others only on this fundamental capitalistic premise: "From Mutual Agreement to Mutual Benefit."

Said differently: Ethically acting (i.e., selfishly motivated) individuals purposefully profit from, i.e., excessively benefit from their voluntarily agreed to social interactions with other selfishly motivated individuals. And the selfish creation of social benefit, that is, the purposeful creation of profit, is described under and by the definition of the concept: ***capitalism***.

Capitalism is evolutionarily different from selfishness. Capitalism is the intellectual advancement over what the metaphysical nature of selfishness is. Capitalism is the epistemological concomitant of selfishness. Capitalism is proper individual behavior moved into a social setting.

Capitalism is not a real something; it is an ideal something. Capitalism is not a physically potent idea; it is an intellectually potent idea. Capitalism does not describe what proper individual behavior is and requires; it describes what a rational social interaction is and requires.

To be a capitalist does not mean to be a person who benefits from one's own individual actions. To be capitalist means to be a person who profits from one's agreed-upon interactions with others. Capitalism describes that naturally occurring social relationship that exists between ethically functioning individuals, between individuals who engage others for no other purpose than to selfishly enjoy even *greater* personal benefits.

Where beneficial action is considered ethical, profitable interaction is considered moral. Restating: Where proper individual action is considered ethical, rational social interaction is considered moral. And where personal selfishness is considered proper, social capitalism is considered rational.

Capitalism does not describe the real production of products, goods, and services; it describes the ideal production of *more* products, goods, and services.

A capitalistic relationship produces greater benefits only for those engaged in it. Otherwise, we need to explain what charity is and requires. And since *charity* is a term described under the idea of religion, it is not proper to include it here under a rational discussion.

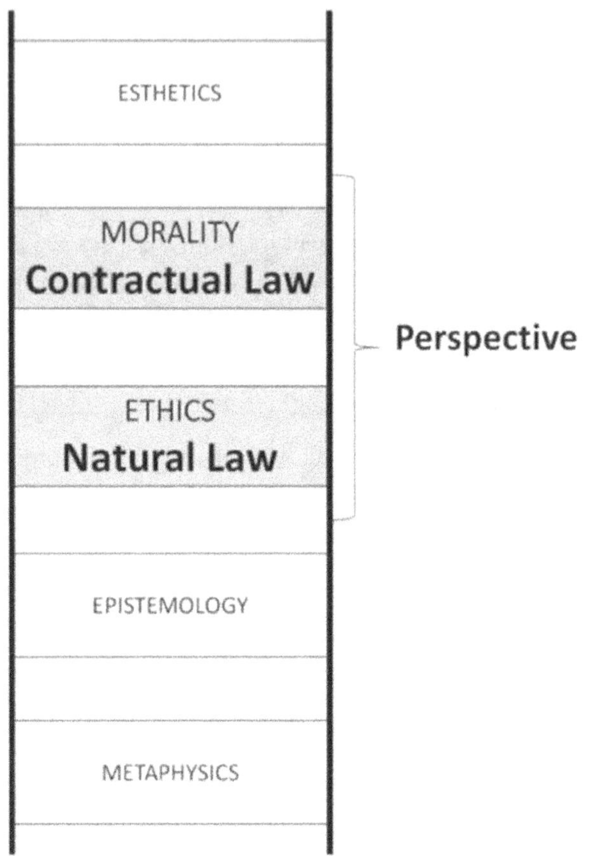

The Ethics of Natural Law

Any action, whether ethical or moral, whether individual or social, whether selfish or capitalistic, whether natural or contractual, carries consequences.

Under ethics, these consequences are called *natural consequences*. Recall that under ethics we are considering an individual who is living alone on a deserted island. The consequences of his actions are delivered to him by the "Laws of Nature." They cannot be avoided. When he performs an action, he will experience the consequence resulting naturally from it.

If he is a properly functioning human being, the consequence will be pleasant. If not, the consequence will be suffering, anguish, sadness, and eventually death.

The Morality of Contractual Law

Repeating from above: Any action, whether ethical or moral, whether individual or social, whether selfish or capitalistic, whether natural or contractual, carries consequences.

Under morality we are considering the consequences resulting from the voluntarily agreed-to social interactions between ethical functioning individuals. These consequences are called *contractual consequences* as opposed to *natural consequences*.

In a rational (a properly functioning) social interaction, the individuals involved in that interaction do not engage one another without first understanding what the consequences resulting from that interaction will be. These consequences are understood and agreed to by each prior to either performing any action. Agreed-to consequences are considered moral and therefore rational as opposed to being considered ethical and therefore proper.

Under the principles of social morality, the consequences of agreed-to interactions are written down and become the *laws of contract*. It is these laws of contract that the idea of capitalism was created to denote the rational nature of. Notice how the laws of man described within, under, and by the idea of capitalism are the moral equivalent of the Laws of Nature governing ethical, i.e., selfishly motivated, behavior performed in a social setting.

Notice that the moral laws of capitalism are a step up from the ethical laws of selfishness. It is therefore impossible for a capitalistic agreement to violate the ethical nature of the persons engaged in it. Contractual law applies the Laws of Nature governing proper human behavior to society.

Social morality is evolutionarily different from personal ethics. Social morality is an epistemological advancement over the metaphysical nature of personal ethics. The idea of social morality represents an intellectual advancement over what the physical nature of the idea of personal ethics is and requires of one's behavior in a social setting.

Responsibility

To behave consequentially, i.e., for one's behavior to be guided by the Laws of Nature determining a proper human existence, requires one to understand what the consequences resulting from one's actions will be prior to performing the virtue that **will** bring those consequences into reality. This is the principle of *responsibility*. Each person is responsible for his own actions, necessarily including the consequences resulting from those actions.

The purpose for legalizing the "Laws of Nature" governing selfish behavior in a social setting is to provide a document that can be witnessed by those concerned with whether they can be considered a properly functioning human being when socially engaged. Their documented witness is testimony of their intent to act in a proper human manner at all times and under all circumstances. The document protects others from their transgressions, whether purposeful or not.

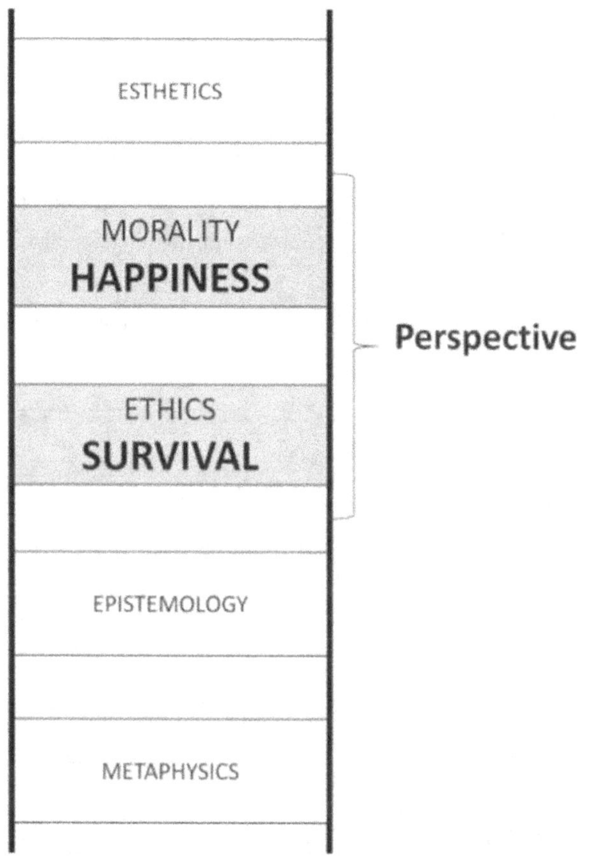

The Ethics of Survival

Under ethics, the Laws of Nature governing what a proper human existence is and requires of one's behavior are the final arbiter as to whether one's actions are beneficial to one's person or not. It is the Laws of Nature that govern whether one's actions are in accordance with what one is and where one is living. Violating natural law carries serious consequences, including death.

If one is behaving properly, then the consequences resulting from one's actions will respect one's fundamental nature as a certain kind of organism, the human one. The only responsibility the person living alone on the deserted island has is to perform those actions that will ensure he remains a living person on that island. The consequence of behaving in accordance with one's nature as a living human being right here on earth has been named, it is called *survival*. This is the principle of personal survival.

As we have seen, to act properly as a human being means to selfishly benefit from one's own actions. The benefit the person living alone on the deserted island enjoys is the continued existence of his living-self. To act for one's continued living existence is to act ethically. To act ethically is to be selfishly motivated to avoid death.

Personal survival is the fundamental underlying principle of ethics. Note that ethics only involves living individuals. It is only living individuals who can act ethically, who can act in accordance with their best interest, who can be selfishly motivated to avoid death.

The person living alone on the deserted island will act in his best interest throughout his entire lifespan, and then he will die. He has no other option. There is no other alternative available to him. His continued existence on that deserted island is governed by the Laws of Nature. The ethical science of philosophy deals only with the survival requirements of individual living persons, and the lifespan of each individual living person is finite. One day it will cease to exist.

The Morality of Happiness

When we integrate the principles of ethical behavior (as governed by the Laws of Nature) with the principles of moral interactions (as *explained* by the idea of Capitalism), we get the Laws of Man. When the Laws of Nature governing ethical behavior are integrated with the laws of man governing moral interactions, we transition from personal survival to social happiness. The difference is immense. It is beyond measure. It is the difference between living properly and surviving death.

Living properly is a time-sensitive idea, whereas surviving death is not.

Under ethics, people act to their personal benefit. But under morality, these same people associate with other ethical people to create an even greater benefit for themselves. As we have seen, that greater personal benefit is called the *profit* resulting naturally from their voluntary social interactions. And the purposeful production of profit is explained under and by the definition of the term *capitalism*.

Have I stressed this point this enough? I have repeated myself on this point—repeatedly. Why? Because capitalism is the most misunderstood and misrepresented idea in the entire English language, even more so than God, which will also soon be cleared up.

Ethical people engage other ethical people for only one reason—to purposefully and excessively benefit from, i.e., to selfishly profit from, that social interaction—and the purposefully selfishly production of profit, i.e., the purposeful creation of excessive personal benefits, is denoted with the term *capitalism*. Properly functioning individuals purposefully capitalize on the talents, skills, and abilities of others. They must. They have no other alternative if they are to be considered properly functioning human beings when socially engaged.

FUNDAMENTAL CAPITALISM!

A fundamental action is that action upon which the success of all others of similar characteristics depend. Fundamentally speaking, then, the profit one enjoys by virtue of one's purposeful social interactions has been named. It is called their **child**.

Their child is of enormous personal benefit to each person involved in a fundamentally capitalistic, i.e., a fundamentally selfish, i.e., a fundamentally moral, i.e., a fundamentally productive social interaction. Their child is their living existence continuing to exist into the future. Their child represents the living existence of each person continuing to exist not anew…but still.

Their child is not different from the living existence of each; it is an extension of the living existence of each. Their child is living physical evidence of, or proof of the continued living existence of each, existing still but as another freestanding living human being.

Where the continued existence of one's own living person is evidence of one's ability to act in an ethically guided, or in a personally responsible selfish manner while socially engaged, the existence of one's child is evidence of one's ability to selfishly, ethically, capitalistically and morally; benefit from the "living existence" of another person.

FUNDAMENTAL CAPITALISM, then, **marries** ethics to morality and conceptualizes it (or intellectualizes it) with the term *LOVE*.

You are living evidence of all those who precede you with their living existence. You are proof that their living existence has not yet gone out of existence. You are living proof that their living existence exists still, but as your own living-self.

To act ethically is to selfishly do that which is required to live a normal lifespan on a deserted island. To act morally is to capitalistically do that which is required for one's life to continue to exist potentially for the remainder of eternity.

Chapter 8

Discussing "The Explanation Group"

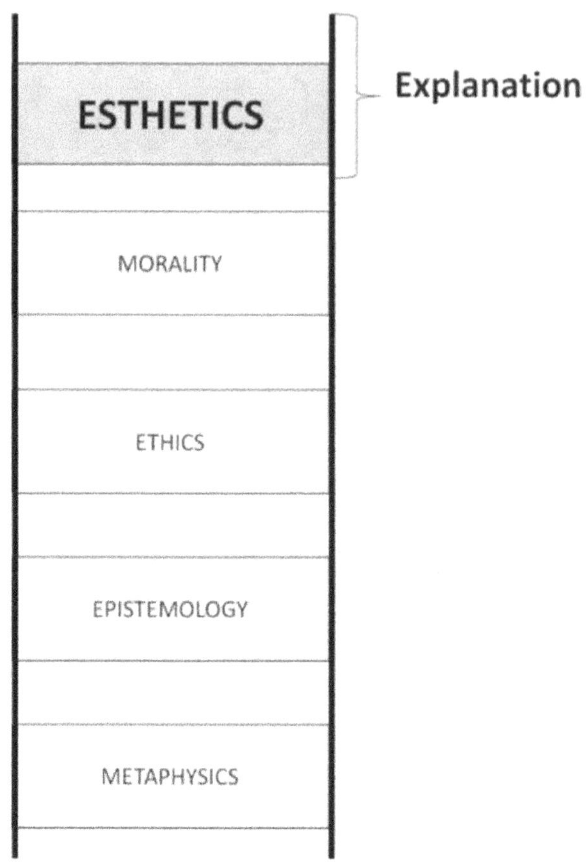
ESTHETICS
Explanation
MORALITY
ETHICS
EPISTEMOLOGY
METAPHYSICS

Devotion to truth is the hallmark of intelligence. A truth is not and can never be, not true, i.e., a truth can never be false. A truth is always true under all conditions and every circumstance. A truth was true for every person who has ever lived at any time in the past. A truth is true for every person who now lives anywhere on the planet regardless of the conditions or the circumstances under which they live. A truth will remain true for every person who will ever live at any time in the future, anyplace in the entire physical universe.

To tell the truth is to behave intellectually, which means to behave as a properly functioning human being while socially engaged. The truth stands *above* the moral rung of the philosophical ladder. To tell the truth requires acknowledgment of the rational nature of human beings. However, not all persons do, or are able to, function rationally, i.e., in accordance with the Laws of Nature governing what a proper human existence is.

Case in point: Suicide bombers and child kidnapping, rapping, murdering, bastards.

It is impossible to formulate a truth in the absence of a properly formulated moral principle. And it is impossible to formulate a moral principle in the absence of a properly formulated ethical principle, which is impossible to formulate in the absence of a properly formulated epistemological principle, which is impossible to formulate in the absence of a properly formulated metaphysical principle.

In other terms, to tell the truth depends on knowing what it is one is talking about. And knowing, as we have seen, is that automatically occurring sensual event that takes place between two real objects when at least one of these objects is a brain.

To tell a truth is to accurately describe one's relationship with some other aspect of physical reality. To tell a truth is to accurately describe, i.e., to explain, that upon which its sensual, factual, conscious, true, perceptual, rational, conceptual, and intellectual nature depends. To tell a truth is to provide to another the "physical" evidence (the proof) required to validate that the truth is a derivation of something one knows to be the case. To tell a truth is to bring into the sensual range of the other that upon which its intellectual nature depends.

To explain the nature of human nature is to tell the truth about what the nature of human nature is. The nature of human nature is governed by the Laws of Nature. It is impossible to tell a truth about (i.e., to explain the true nature of) human nature outside the Laws of Nature governing that upon which a proper human existence depends right here on earth.

Meaning that it is impossible to tell the truth about **God** outside the Laws of Nature governing human happiness right here on earth. The issue is not "Does God exist?" Nor is it "What is God?" The issue is "Why does God exist?"

Why did the human mind create God and therefore must be held responsible for bringing God into existence right here on earth?

The Philosophical Ladder Revisited

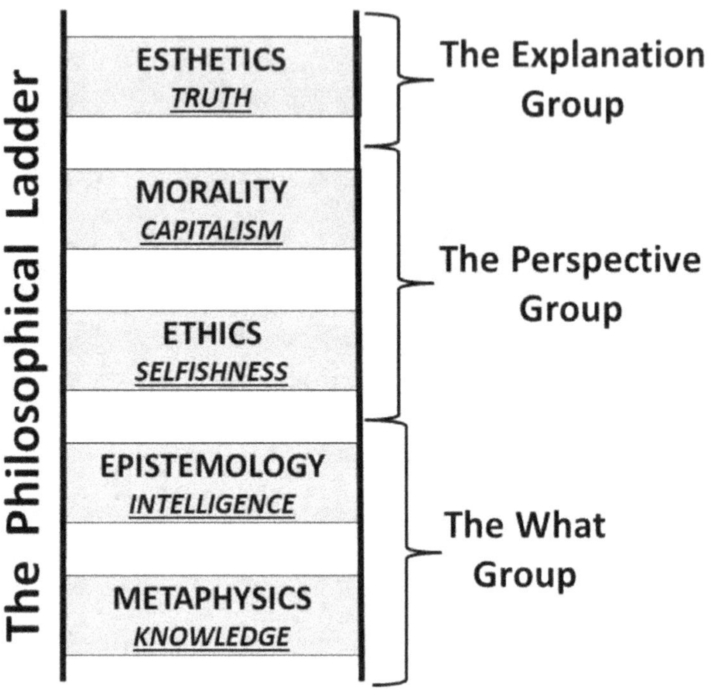

The final group of the philosophical ladder is "The Explanation Group." This group consists of a single rung, the esthetics rung. The esthetical rung of The Philosophy of Explanation is that science concerned with explaining the true nature of human happiness and that upon which its continued existence right here on earth depends. To explain human happiness, i.e., to tell the truth about what constitutes human happiness, requires there are living humans to explain it to.

To explain something is to reveal that it is what it is, that it does exist in a verifiable manner. To tell the truth about (i.e., to explain the nature of) human happiness and that upon which its continued existence depends requires one to be standing firmly on the esthetical rung of the philosophical ladder. To firmly stand on the esthetical rung of philosophical ladder requires one to have previously stood firmly on the moral rung of the philosophical ladder. To have firmly stood on the moral rung requires one to have previously stood firmly on the ethical rung. To have firmly stood on the ethical rung requires one to have previously stood firmly on the epistemological rung. To have firmly stood on the epistemological rung requires one to have previously stood firmly on the metaphysical rung.

It's impossible to tell the truth about, i.e., to explain, the true nature of human happiness until one has satisfied each rung of the philosophical ladder. Alternately, it is impossible to explain, i.e., to tell the truth about, the true nature of human happiness until one has advanced up the philosophical ladder from the bottom to the top.

It is impossible to tell the truth about, and thereby to explain, the true nature of human happiness until one can explain the Laws of Nature as these apply to and derive the laws of a moral-functioning society. The laws of a moral-functioning society are derived from those naturally occurring Laws of Nature governing what a proper human existence consists of and requires for it to continue to happily exist. This is saying that the laws of a moral-functioning society can only be developed by observing the actions of ethically functioning individuals when those individuals are socially engaged. The laws of ethical behavior translated into the laws of moral behavior become the "proper" laws of society.

The laws of personal survival are determined by man's animal nature; the laws of social happiness are determined by man's intellectual nature. One cannot be separated from the other. The laws of social happiness are evolutionarily different from the laws of personal survival. They are an intellectual expansion of, i.e., they are an epistemological expansion of, what one's personal happiness requires of one. Ethical behavior is a necessity of personal survival; ethical behavior in a social setting is a necessity of social happiness. The laws of social happiness are captured under the concept of capitalism.

Capitalism, then, is the fundamental requirement for social happiness to exist.

Capitalism is a derivation of social morality, which is a derivation of personal ethics, which is a derivation of human intelligence, which is a derivation of human survival, which is a derivation of the Laws of Nature. It's impossible to explain (to tell the truth about) a reason-based philosophy in any other manner.

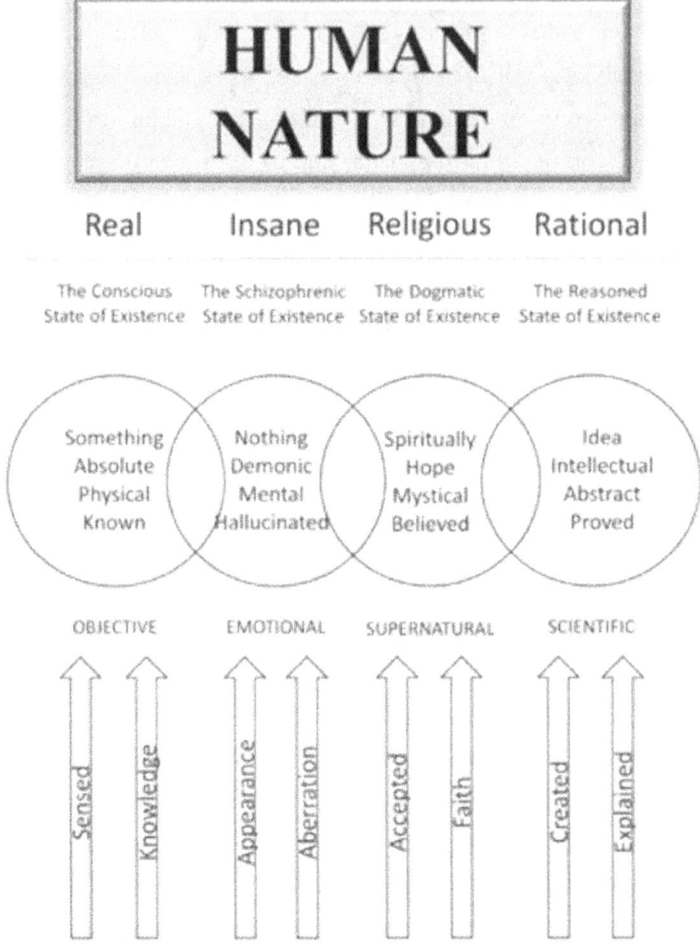

Recall when we previously discussed this "Human Nature" graphic.

Recall that we discussed the premise that to become intellectual, one needs to fully remove oneself from the stupefying influence of religion on one's mind. I will now continue this discussion, but first I will remove the insane and the religious alternatives from the above "Human Nature" graphic resulting in the below graphic.

If one were searching for why the Space Shuttle exists and one went to an insane asylum to conduct that research, one's efforts would be frustrated by what one finds there. Similarly, as one searches for the requirements of human happiness here on earth but remains connected to, and thereby influenced by, the underlying principles of religion, one's efforts will likewise be frustrated by what one finds.

This is because the dogmatic nature of religion is a purposeful attempt to explain the existence of nothing as if were not nothing. As such, dogmatic religion is not different from what mental insanity is. It is merely the mystical (not intellectual) expansion of it. Whenever we remain connected to a fundamentally insane religious premise that will frustrate our intellectual efforts. One cannot pursue intelligence religiously, only rationally.

For one to discover why humans have remained in existence for as long as they have, right here on earth (in reality) one need only observe the consequences resulting from ethical-acting individuals when they are socially engaged. It is only persons who act in a properly selfish (ethical) manner, in a social setting, that can be held responsible for the continued existence of happy human beings right here on earth.

This is how you got here, this is how I got here, and this is how the human species can continue to exist in reality for perhaps the remainder of eternity.

Note that the idea of eternity is not a time-sensitive idea. Therefore, the idea of **eternal-survival** is the concept of *individual-survival* absent its misplaced time requirement. To eternally survive is to always exist. And to always exist requires that time is not involved in that existence. "Eternal-time" is a contradiction.

To survive requires that the living ***existence*** of one's life does not cease to exist ever.

Time is a concept created by the human mind. Time is not real, it is ideal. Time does not exist in reality; it exists in human intelligence. The issue is not "What is time?" nor is it "Does time exist?" The issue is "Why does time exist?" "Why did the human mind create time and therefore, must be held responsible for bringing time into existence right here on earth?"

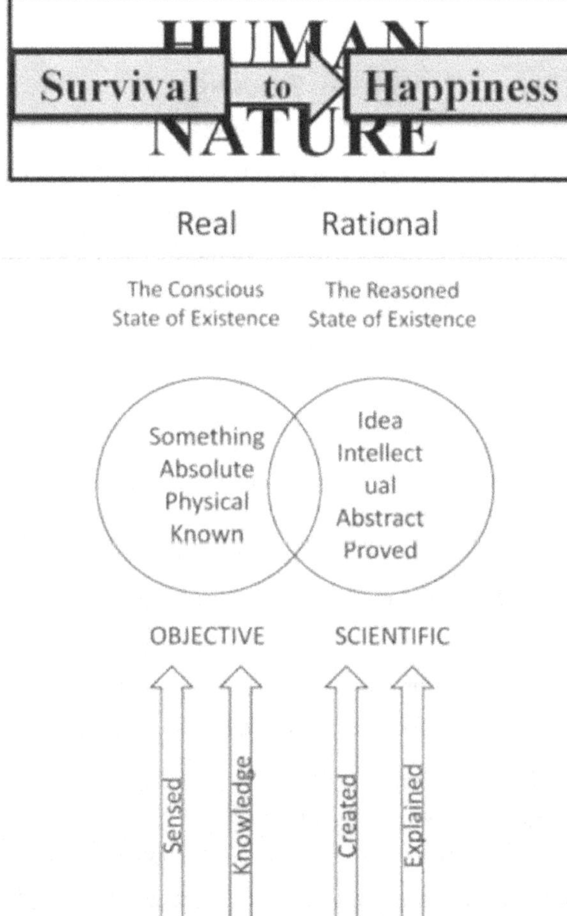

When insanity, and its religious counterpart, is removed from the discussion, we are left with the above "Human Nature" graphic. We now have only the real, and its rational counterpart, as the focus of our discussion. This altered structure permits us to examine the nature of human nature more closely for the specific purpose of understanding happiness and that upon which its continued existence depends.

If one were to closely investigate the above graphic, one would find that the real alternative is the basis of ethics and that the rational alternative is the basis of morality. Further investigation of it would reveal that only ethical persons do act properly, and only moral persons can achieve happiness.

ETHICAL BEHAVIOR
(Personal Survival)

Under the laws of human nature, and therefore under the principles of ethics, is where we talk about personal survival. To survive means to remain a living being, which requires remaining alive. Notice that survival does not and cannot include death. This is because to die is to fail to survive death.

Like eternity, personal survival is not a time-sensitive idea. Survival does not mean temporary existence; it means permanent existence. To survive death means to not die, ever! But notice how this seems to contradict that which one sensually knows to be the case. Let me emphasize that the contradiction only *seems* to exist. The evidence is otherwise.

The eternal nature of one's life is an idea based in what one already knows to be the case but may not have thought much about. I am going to uncover and resolve that thinking failure. The failure to identify, and from there, to explain what is sensually known to be the case with regard to the eternal nature of the permanent existence of one's own life.

When we focus on the needs of our physical being, as the beasts do, we are constrained by what is available to our sensual observation. We do observe that individual human persons do die. I do not dispute this observation. It is a good, true, and valid observation. Individual humans do die. All humans will eventually die. All animals will eventually die. All plants will eventually die. I cannot and do not, and therefore will not, dispute this observation.

To discuss the issue of human happiness we must move the discussion from the real to the ideal, from the physical to the rational, from the objective to the conceptual, from sensual knowing to reasoned understanding, from personal selfishness to social capitalism, from timed existence to eternal existence, from religion to intelligence.

As previously discussed, social happiness is the epistemological concomitant of personal survival moved into a social setting. Where *survival* is a concept based in the eternal nature of physical reality, *happiness* is a concept based in the rational nature of human intelligence. Where survival involves knowing that one's life exists, happiness involves understanding what the existence of one's life requires of one's actions for it to "always" remain in existence. Note that successfully satisfying the needs of one's life while living on a deserted island is wrongfully termed <u>survival</u> because one's life processes will eventually stop functioning. In this specific case, "surviving happily" on a deserted island carries an intellectually important internal contradiction.

The intellectual experience resulting from understanding that one has successfully put into place the conditions required for one's life to continue to exist is properly called happiness. One's existence is a physically potent idea, where one's happiness is an intellectually potent idea. However, one cannot be separated from the other.

To explain the requirements of happiness requires one to understand the cause-and-effect relationship existing between behavior and consequences, between acting as a beast and acting as a human, between acting religiously and acting intellectually. Where acting intellectually (in accordance with the Laws of Nature) involves reason, acting religiously (in accordance with the laws of faith) involves emotion. Achieving happiness requires reason, not emotion. Emotion (religious or otherwise) will get in the way of one's achievement of happiness.

To achieve happiness, one must be able to understand that there is an alternative to one's eternal death and that one is able to experience it. But to stop here is to fail. One must do that which is a requirement of avoiding eternal death; otherwise, one will not experience it. One must behave consequentially; one must purposefully create the conditions required for one's life to continue to exist even beyond one's physical death. When that has occurred, the result is intellectual happiness. This requires one to think about what the requirements of achieving intellectual happiness are and to then to put into action those virtues required to bring about a happy experience.

I am frequently asked, "Do you believe you are going to die?" I respond with "No! I know I am going to die." But this is, of course, not a completely accurate "intellectual" response. And the reason for this is that "knowing is that automatically occurring sensual response between two things when at least one of these things is a brain." In other terms, I have not sensually witnessed my own physical death. Therefore, the claim "No! I know I am going to die" is not based on what I know to be the case. The accurate way to respond to such a question would be "No! I *understand*, after considering all the available evidence, that one day I will die."

Knowing how to survive is beastly, understanding the purpose of one's existence and how to realize that purpose right here on earth is human. Beasts instinctively respond to (emotionally react to) painful and pleasurable experiences, Humans intellectually understand the cause-and-effect relationships naturally resulting in painful and pleasurable experiences.

Understanding cause-and-effect relationships is that mental action called conceptual reasoning. Recall that thinking is the virtue of reason. Conceptual reasoning is that purposefully performed mental action responsible for translating reality into intelligence as terms (words and concepts) and their definitions.

When one understands that one's physical death does not necessarily require that the existence of one's life ceases to exist, this understanding will have an evolutionary effect on the way one thinks and therein on the way one behaves. This is saying that when investigating human happiness and what it requires, one cannot be limited by what is sensually available to one's beastly brain. That investigation must also include that which one's human mind understands about the eternal nature of that naturally occurring and self-sustaining energy of the universe now trapped within the cellular structure of one's body which has been purposefully re-termed into **life**. The energy of the universe exists naturally and eternally, that exact same energy, now existing within the cells of a human body, exists purposefully and dependently. Meaning that the continued existence of the eternal nature of human life is dependent on the rational nature of the mind controlling the purposefully performed actions of that body.

All organisms selfishly, meaning purposefully, act to support, protect, maintain, and promote their life processes into the future, potentially forever!

When investigating happiness, the requirement is to understand why human beings must, and therefore do, achieve their purpose. With that purpose being to be the cause of their life remaining in existence, potentially forever.

We need to understand the intellectual nature of human nature rather than just knowing that human beings do exist. Once we understand why properly functioning humans must act in the ways they do, we can then begin to understand what human happiness is and that upon which its continued existence, right here on earth, depends.

Intelligence is not a concern for **what** one's existence is; intelligence is the consequence resulting from understanding **why** it does, i.e., what the cause of one's intelligence is. *You* and *I* and *they* do exist. That is what we need to be talking about. What is that? It is the *existence* of our and their living existence and what that requires of our behavior for it to remain in existence, perhaps for the remainder of eternity.

Fundamentally speaking: One's responsibility (as the intellectual animal) is to think about, and from there to understand, and from there to explain, why one's life exists and what its existence requires of one's behavior (physically, intellectually, and emotionally) prior to one considering oneself to be a properly functioning human being—right here on earth.

EXISTENCE

Existence is the first term, i.e., the fundamental term, of intelligence. Ayn Rand referred to "existence" as being an axiomatic concept. She defined an axiom in this manner:

> *"An **axiom** is an irreducible truth expressed in the form of a proposition. A truth you cannot prove nor do without. Axioms are self-evident concepts that form the basis for all higher-level knowledge."*

Existence denotes the existence of the transition point existing between nothing and everything. Existence is not a something the nature of which is physically potent in the manner of a rock and therefore the existence of existence cannot be sensually known to exist. Existence, then, is not objective, it is conceptual; meaning that it is not real, it is intellectual. Existence exists as a term the purpose of which it to intellectually denote (or to audio/visually "stand in the place of") the existence of the absolute nature of physical reality. It, therefore, does not have (and cannot have) a definition. Existence exists only because the mind function of the human brain created it; and therefore, must be held responsible for bringing existence into existence right here on earth. The intellectual nature of the existence of existence can only be understood to exist by the mind function of the human brain.

Unlike non-axiomatic terms which are abstractions based on something which is sensually known to exist; the axiomatic nature of **existence** has no sensually potent physical referent. Its existence is purely intellectual, i.e., it is axiomatic.

An example: "Water" is an intellectual abstraction based on the previously sensually known existence of a real physical something. Note that it is important to recognize that the existence of that real "something" *pre-existed* the creation of the term water audio/visually denoting the existence of its physical characteristics.

The term "existence," on the other hand; was created in the absence of the sensually known existence of an existing real physical referent. Therefore, the intellectual nature of existence is considered axiomatic rather than conceptual. Again: To exist axiomatically is to exist as an intellectual transition point between the existence of nothing (i.e., as an absurdity) and the existence of everything (i.e., as a truth).

Absent intelligence, there is no way for the existence of existence to be understood to have been brought into existence by the intellectual nature of the mind function of the human brain.

It can be said that existence exists, and that intelligence is evidence of it. Intelligence is what the *existence* of the absolute nature of physical reality becomes when conceptualized into one's mind as terms and their definitions by the intellectual nature of the mind considering the existence of the intellectual nature of itself.

Happiness is the term denoting the existence of that naturally occurring intellectual response resulting from one's understanding of what the fundamental value of the *existence* of the life of one's child means for the future existence of one's own life.

The issue boils down to this: Every living organism will eventually die. But does that, as if by the law of necessity, demand that its living existence has gone out of existence? The evidence is clear, and the answer is no! What is the evidence supporting such a claim? It is the living existence of you, me, and them!

Consider this: If it is true that every person preceding you has died, in the sense their living existence has gone out of existence, then how do you explain your living-existence? If their living existence has gone out of existence, why are you here? Where do you think your living-existence came from?

A theist will tell you that your living existence exists because of the miraculous powers of their God-being. But your mind understands this is not the case. Your mind understands that you have parents and that it is their actions, as properly functioning living beings, which is responsible for why *their* living existence exists—still as your living existence. Your mind understands that your living existence is not different from that of your parents. Your mind understands this, but it may not, as yet, have thought about the enormous implication this will have on your intelligence, and thereby on your behavior, once your mind does begin to think about it.

When your mind begins to understand that your living existence exists and that there is a way by which you can cause it to continue to exist, even beyond your own personal lifespan, this understanding will set your mind free of the mystical influence religious belief may now enjoy over its rational operations.

Acknowledge this: Unlike the knowing function of your brain, the understanding function of its mind, called reasoning, does not proceed automatically. Thinking (the virtue of reason) is that mind function that must be done, i.e., it must be volitionally engaged. If your mind is to ever begin to think, you are the one who must cause it to do that. I cannot cause you to think; no one can. That is your intellectual responsibility as a properly functioning human being to think about what you are, where you are living, and what these require of your physical, intellectual, and emotional behavior prior to considering *yourself* to be a properly functioning human being.

To survive means to do that which your nature as a living being requires of you. A person living alone on a deserted island can be considered a properly functioning, ethical-guided, selfishly motivated person, but he cannot be considered a rational functioning, morally guided, capitalistically motivated member of society. Recall that it is the consequences resulting naturally from one's voluntary social interactions that determine whether one's actions are moral.

Notice how our island dweller can only do that which is required to live throughout a normal lifespan. He cannot do that which is required for his living existence to continue to survive beyond his own physical death. He can selfishly benefit from his ethical actions, but he cannot capitalistically profit by purposefully offering the fundamental value of his life to another. This is because a profitable social interaction is not available to him, and this is because he is the only person living on that deserted island.

Personal production is the fundamental requirement for the existence of one's life to continue to exist beyond one's lifespan. The law of fundamentality applied to one's living existence states that personal production is that ethical act upon which the continued existence of (perhaps eternal survival of) one's living-self depends. To be considered personally productive requires there is another with whom one has been socially involved with an equal other.

Personal production is where ethics and morality become one and the same. Personal production is the intellectual conduit differentiating ethical survival from moral happiness. Personal production is the intellectual conduit differentiating living properly from existing eternally. Ethics requires one to benefit from one's behavior. Morality states that the fundamental benefit resulting from one's selfishly motivated behavior cannot be realized until one has been capitalistically engaged with another selfishly motivated equal.

Do not become confused by what is being said here. This is not saying that people who do not, for whatever reason, have children cannot be considered functioning in a proper human way. That would be an absurdity. What is being said here is that they cannot be considered to be happy about that.

The contrary of happiness is sorrow. It is not possible to experience sorrow in the absence of a real cause of it. As happiness is an intellectual abstraction, so is sorrow. Since happiness and sorrow are intellectual abstractions, then, they are not sensual knowns. What they are, what their *true* meaning is, can only be understood.

Like all intellectual abstractions, that which is responsible for the true meaning of the term happiness begins with a sensual know. Recall that "knowing is that automatically occurring sensual response between two objects when at least one of these objects is a brain." These types of automatically occurring sensual responses are more properly called "instinctual reactions." Like all non-human animals, the beasts, instinctual responses to pain and pleasure are also requirements of proper human survival. Fundamentally speaking, humans are also properly considered to be selfishly motivated beasts, excepting that humans have a single additional identifying characteristic conceptualized with the term-mind. It is the reasoning power of the mind function of one's own brain that permits one to consider oneself to be a human animal rather than just another beastly animal which; of course, one also is.

Within the mind function of the human brain a painful physical experience is the responsible cause of the concept of sorrow and a pleasurable physical experience is the responsible cause of the concept of happiness.

When I watched my daughter Kristin being born that made me happy, very happy. I didn't care to, nor did I need to, understand *why*. Being happy does not need to be understood or explained. This is because happiness is the normal state of existence for the mind function of a properly functioning human brain.

But—when I watched her die all the rules changed. I *needed* to understand that. It wasn't something I wanted to do. It was something I had to do. I had no option as to how I responded to watching my baby die. The issue was, either understand it or go insane. Going insane is the intellectual equivalent of physical death. This remains the most serious issue I have ever faced. I cried every single day for twenty years before I got to a place where I understood just what the *hell* had happened to me—personally. I am not happy because of what I have discovered. But now I do understand my sorrow. I understand why the pain is so intense and so overpowering and why it will never go away, and most importantly, why I do not want it to ever go away.

Happiness is not real; it is ideal. Happiness is not something one can go to a market and purchase a gallon of. Happiness is not a something that exists in a physical kind of way. Happiness is a necessity for the continued existence of human-based life forms right here on earth, i.e., here in reality. Happiness does not occur automatically just because one has done whatever one dammed well pleases. Happiness is the natural result of a specific human act, the purposeful production of one's living-self into the future for a long as possible. And that purpose is called happiness. Notice how happiness cannot be achieved via hope, religious or otherwise; it can only be achieved via the purposeful, selfishly motivated reproduction of self.

When one's living-self exists again as another freestanding human being, one properly renames the "second coming" of one's living-self into one's living **child-self**. One's living child-self is evidence of; it is proof of, the "second coming" of one's living-self.

The term "offspring" means exactly what it implies. It means that one's living-self has "sprung away" from one's body and in doing so becomes one's living-self existing not again, but still, as another freestanding living person whom one properly re-terms into being one's child-self.

The tragedy is that many people are happy and don't realize it. And many people claim to be happy and have no idea what it is they are talking about. The greater tragedy is that many people deserve personal happiness but are unable to achieve it.

My own daughter, Kristin, is an example of this.

CHAPTER 10

*Explaining How the God of Capitalism Is Considered
to Be the Responsible Cause of Human Happiness Right Here on Earth*

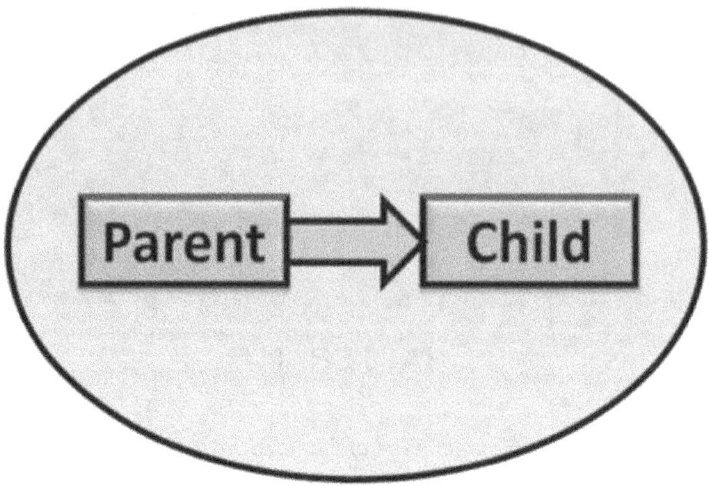

The idea described by the concept of capitalism does not address why human happiness exists, in abundance, on this planet. Capitalism was not created to address the issue of happy human existence. Capitalism was created only to describe how properly functioning persons behave when socially engaged; they behave morally. In other terms, capitalism discusses that behavior the natural outcome of which is the *proper* existence of human beings while socially engaged. It does not discuss that behavior, the natural outcome of which is the *happy* existence of individual human beings, potentially, for the remainder of eternity.

As implied above there is a special kind of capitalistic behavior that is responsible for why human happiness exists in abundance on this planet. But to avoid a great deal of confusion, we must replace the term *capitalism* whenever we discuss the selfishly motivated production of human happiness. That new term is **God**. Like capitalism, God also describes ethical, i.e., selfishly motivated, behavior while socially engaged. God is the new term replacing capitalism whenever discussing the real cause of the eternal nature of human happiness.

Herein is the reasoned development of the idea *"**The God of Capitalism**."*

Since God is a more fundamental term than capitalism, i.e., since God came into the human language prior to capitalism, then, whenever we use the term *God* it is not proper to continue to use the newer capitalistic term *profit*. The new term replacing profit is **CHILD**.

Where *capitalism* is that idea focused on the survival needs of the individuals of which society consists of, *God* is that special capitalistic idea focused on the eternal needs of the life processes of those same individuals. It is the selfish production of profit that capitalism describes. It is the happy production of children that God describes. However, each is a requirement of the continued living existence of happy human beings right here on earth.

The child of God replaces the profit of capitalism whenever discussing human happiness.

Notice how when pursuing God, it is no longer proper to claim we are behaving in a capitalistic manner. To avoid confusion when discussing that special pre-capitalistic activity responsible for the happy production of **children,** we have transitioned from acting in a capitalistic manner to behaving in a Godly manner.

We are the source of the happiness our parents experienced in the same way our children are the source of the happiness we experience. We have reproduced the happiness our parents experienced by reproducing that which is responsible for it: our living selves. For our parents, the product resulting from our selfish pursuit of the children of God is called their grandchild. Whenever we successfully act in a godly manner, we are the ones responsible for extending their happiness into the future.

Very importantly, one's child is not something new in the sense that it came from nothing. One's child is one's living existence that continues to exist—still. One's child is living evidence of one's living existence existing not *anew*; but *still*. Fundamentally, one's child is one's living existence existing not again; but still, as a separate freestanding living person.

Notice we have again advanced the discussion, and this requires us to change the terms we use. To avoid confusion when discussing the purposeful God-driven creation of one's child-self, we can no longer use the newer capitalistic idea of *social interaction*. The pre-capitalistic term used to explain one's Godly motivated behavior is *sexual intercourse*. Sexual intercourse replaces the idea of social interaction whenever we discuss how and why happy humans continue to exist right here on earth. Sexual intercourse is the fundamental moral idea because it is the fundamental ethical requirement. Recall that ethics requires that individual persons benefit from their own selfishly motivated actions. The greatest benefit a fundamentally selfish person, i.e., a person of God, can enjoy is the continued existence of one's living-self as one's living ***child-self***.

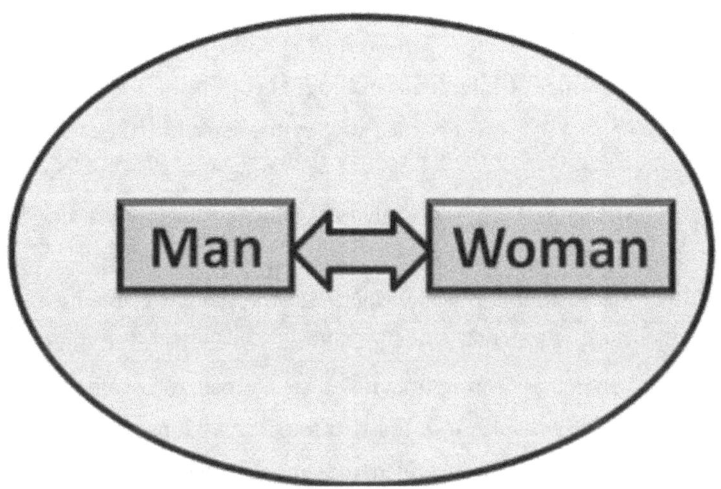

The Truth About the Real Nature of God Is Now Available

God was created by the human mind to denote (or to intellectually "stand in the place of") that special capitalistic relationship that can only exist between a man and a woman.

Where capitalism describes the fundamental requirements for the social production of profit, the **God** of capitalism describes the fundamental requirements for the social production of The Children of God. With the child of God replacing the profit of Capitalism whenever discussing "human" happiness.

A capitalistic interaction produces that which is a requirement of individual living human beings remaining alive throughout a normal lifespan. A Godly interaction produces that which is the requirement for the life processes of those same individual living human beings remaining in existence, potentially for the remainder of eternity, right here on earth. God is the basis of what profit-motivated behavior is, i.e., of what a fundamentally selfishly motivated, ethically guided, beastly behavior is, while socially engaged.

Capitalism produces *more* goods, products, and services. God produces *more* humans.

Under the idea of ethics, we discuss what a properly functioning human being is and requires. Under the idea of morality, we discuss what a rational functioning society is and requires. Under the idea of capitalism, we discuss how ethical individuals interact throughout a normal lifespan. Under the idea of God, we discuss how capitalistic individuals can avoid eternal death.

The capitalistic God is where individual ethics and social morality become one and the same.

However: One cannot ethically experience the God of Capitalism; one can only morally experience the God of Capitalism. Notice that even thou behaving in a proper human manner throughout his entire lifespan, the island dweller is not able to personally experience **God**. For that to occur we must introduce another selfishly motivated, i.e., ethically guided, individual onto the island. However, for either to continue to be considered a properly behaving individual (while socially engaged), each must continue to behave in an ethically guided. i.e., selfishly motivated, manner while socially involved. When successful each will benefit "excessively" from their agreed-to social engagement. Meaning each will have purposefully joined their life with the life of the other in order for their life to continue to enjoy eternal existence. Therein being the development of the idea that each has morally profited, in an "excessive" manner, from the eternal nature of the life of their well-chosen partner. While at the exact same time having selfishly benefited from the eternal nature of one's own life. Meaning that one has become the savior of one's own life as it exists within one's sperm or egg while at the exact same time becoming the savior of the life of one's well-chosen partner in life as it alternately exists within their sperm or egg.

A moral-functioning society can continue to exist only when the individuals of whom it consists of are happy.

We note that the smallest society consists of two persons. If we were to discuss two people living together on a deserted island, we would be able to discuss what a moral-functioning society is and that upon which its continued happy existence depends. And in doing so, we would discover the answer to one of the greatest questions facing man. What is eternal salvation and upon what does it depend?

Eternal Salvation Via Human Love

Note: One's eternal salvation is not achieved and cannot be achieved in isolation. When one understands one is worthy of eternal salvation, one's thoughts and thereby one's actions will be fundamentally altered.

An ethical person, a person selfishly motivated to survive beyond their physical death, will seek another person similarly motivated to survive beyond their physical death. When successful, the living existence of each is saved, possibly forever! Their eternal salvation is provided to them by their selfishly motivated, capitalistically guided Godly interactions. That is, by their mutually agreed-to reproduction of their living-self into their living child-self. Notice how it is their godly behavior that is responsible for the "*second coming*" of their living-self and not the other way around.

Notice how each becomes their own personal savior while at the exact same time becoming the savior of their well-chosen partner in life. It is their capitalistically guided, God based, social interactions described by the concept of <u>sexual intercourse</u> that is responsible for causing or putting into place that which is required for the "existence of their living-self" (reconceptualized under the term **life**) to continue to exist beyond its normal lifespan right here on earth, and possibly for the remainder of eternity.

To love another is to morally acknowledge the Godly nature of the supreme value of the others life. To love one's child-self is to ethically acknowledge the Godly nature of the "second coming" of the supreme value of one's *own life* as it exists not again; but still, as the life of one's child-self. And theirs! And theirs! Etc.—*forever*!

It is the life of one's child-self that proves to one that one has achieved one's purpose right here on earth. With that purpose being achieved only because one has excessively profited from that selfishly motivated behavior described by and under the idea conceptualized as purpose driven sexual intercourse as that is defined under and by the idea conceptualized under the term "the **God** of capitalism."

When one applies the power of one's reason to understanding the fundamental purpose of all living beings (including human beings), one will eventually discover that it is one's **LIFE** that establishes the guideposts for that understanding to occur. Absent one's life, nothing else matters.

Purposefully invoking that behavior described by and under the idea conceptualized as "the *God* of capitalism" is the only behavior that can ensure that one has put into place that which is required for the eternal nature of one's life to continue to eternally exist: And for one to experience the intellectual happiness which acknowledging that as a truth naturally engenders. The God of capitalism describes that behavior which successfully marries the eternal nature of one's life with the eternal nature of the life of another-for one purpose. With that purpose being to be the cause of the eternal nature of one's life continuing to eternally exist.

The God of Capitalism Has Nothing at All to Do with Religious Belief And Everything to Do with Reasoned Intelligence.

"Love of self" <u>conceptualizes</u> the purposefully selfish nature of one's love of one's life back into intelligence as the term…***self-esteem***…and in doing so makes any reference to "the love of a Deity God" obsolete, unnecessary, and (under certain conditions) dangerous. *Self-esteem* is fundamentally moral because it is the fundamental ethical requirement. It is self-esteem that will eventually commit "the love of a Deity God" to the ever-growing scrap heap of religious belief. In doing so, religious belief will eventually become obsolete due to lack of interest.

However: Until the human mind has fully evolved into a fail-proof reasoning organ; the other still beastly behaving humans will continue to emotionally (and therefore dangerously) enforce their absurd beliefs onto those of us who ignore their anti-intellectual behavior—to our peril.

One's love of the life of an another describes that intellectual ***bond*** existing between individuals seeking the truth about the fundamental nature of their human mind. The truth is that it is the mind function of the human brain that is responsible for why properly functioning individuals will continue to behave in their personal best interest, for the remainder of eternity, while socially engaged.

<u>Whatever the hell that means! The proof I offer to you…is you!</u>

Selfishly Motivated Personal Happiness Is Why You Exist

As are you, so is your child
A Child of God.